THE REMARKABLE WORLD OF
FRANCES BARKLEY

THE REMARKABLE WORLD OF

Frances Barkley

1769 - 1845

BETH HILL
WITH CATHY CONVERSE

TOUCHWOOD EDITIONS

VICTORIA • VANCOUVER

TouchWood Editions Ltd.
Victoria, BC, Canada
This book is distributed by The Heritage Group, #108-17665 66A Avenue, Surrey,
BC, Canada, V3S 2A7. www.heritagehouse.ca

Cover painting: Harry Heine, courtesy of Gordon Cooper. Cover design: Marketing
Dynamics. Book design: Retta Moorman. Layout: Katherine Hale.
This book is set in AGaramond.

TouchWood Editions acknowledges the financial support for its publishing program
from The Canada Council for the Arts, the Government of Canada through the Book
Publishing Industry Development Program (BPIDP) and the Province of British Columbia through the British Columbia Arts Council.

Printed and bound in Canada by Friesens, Altona, Manitoba.

National Library of Canada Cataloguing in Publication Data

Barkley, Frances, b. 1769.
    The remarkable world of Frances Barkley, 1769-1845 / Beth Hill and Cathy
Converse. — Expanded ed.

Includes bibliographical references and index.
ISBN 1-894898-08-7

1.Barkley, Frances, b. 1769. 2.Seafaring life. 3.Voyages around the world.
4.British Columbia—Description and travel. 5.Ship captains' spouses—Biography.
I. Hill, Beth, 1924-1997 II. Converse, Cathy, 1944- III. Title.

FC3821.1.B37A3 2003   910.4'1   C2003-905122-6

The Canada Council | Le Conseil des Arts
    for the Arts | du Canada

BRITISH
COLUMBIA
ARTS COUNCIL
We acknowledge the support of the Province of British Columbia
through the British Columbia Arts Council

Dedication

to Beth Hill, 1924 to 1997
writer, researcher and friend, who left us too soon

Acknowledgments

I am grateful to all the Barkley descendants who gave advice, information and encouragement, and I am hoping that the publication of this book will lead to the discovery of the lost Diary of Frances Barkley. I will be delighted to hear from anyone with suggestions related to this quest. Commander George Barkley Barnes, the present owner of the *Reminiscences*, has given his wholehearted approval from the inception of the project.

The many friends who have contributed cannot all be listed here, but I would like to especially thank Jim Whittingham for his excellent drawings, Mary Williamson for much more than the typing, Miles Acheson, Pat Wright and Hilary Stewart. My husband, Ray Hill, accompanying me in the English journeys, did all the careful photography of buildings, books and hundreds of documents, has produced many of the illustrations in this book and has given me his unfailing support. Our son John gave assistance at a critical moment and I appreciate them both.

To the many institutions and individuals who assisted me (the bulging file of correspondence is impressive) I wish to express my gratitude. I am especially indebted to Mr. Allan Turner and the staff of the British Columbia Archives.

Beth Hill, 1978

I would like to thank my husband, Captain Brian Silvester, master mariner, for his patient explanation of sailing routes, currents, winds, ship stability and all other things nautical; Captain John Anderson, master mariner, for providing information on the history of ships' discipline; Bodo De Lange Boom of the Canadian Hydrographic Service Pacific Region and Janet Mason, B.C. Provincial Toponymist, for providing information on Barkley Sound and on confirming the naming of Trevor Channel after Frances Barkley.

Cathy Converse, 2003

Contents

Preface to the First Edition

Anyone may visit the British Columbia Archives in Victoria, British Columbia, and examine Frances Barkley's *Reminiscences*. You fill out a slip and place it in a box on the wide desk which guards the doors leading to the books. An attendant will take your slip, examine it, nod to you and then disappear into the archives beyond the doors. You wait. In the thickly carpeted reading room heads are bent over small tables, and in the silence you can hear the soft fluttery whispers of papers and pages, and the occasional rasp of microfilm turned on the spool. Then, suddenly, the doors swing and the attendant has returned and is handing you a thin, faded notebook with a pale, oiled-paper cardboard cover, and you hold in your hand the memories of Frances Barkley.

I knew almost nothing about her when I first opened that notebook. At the time I was planning to write an article about the petroglyph pictures of sailing ships carved into the sloping sandstone of a beach near Clo-oose, on Vancouver Island's Pacific coast, and I was hoping that it might be possible to identify these ships, to say "This one is Captain Cook's *Resolution,* and this one is Captain Barkley's *Imperial Eagle*" and so on. To make such assertions I had to know the rigging of the first European vessels to reach our shores, and it was during this research that I found the little notebook which Frances filled with memories when she was 66 years old. I was only searching for information for my petroglyph-ship article, but when I began to read the pale ink, it was as if the notebook had been waiting for me. Some connection was made, some trap clicked shut, and Frances Barkley began to take over my life.

At that time I knew only that she was 18 years old when she came to the British Columbian coast in 1787, on her honeymoon, the first European woman to step out upon the smooth sand of our western beaches. How little I suspected, that day

Rubbing of a petroglyph ship at Clo-oose, west coast of Vancouver Island.

in the hushed reading room in Victoria, that in a few months I would be standing in Bridgwater in Somerset beside the font where Frances and her short-lived twin sister were baptized, that I would kneel in the ancient country church at Otterhampton where her young mother had been buried, that I would walk on pavements in Bath, in London, in Hertford, where her feet had pressed the same pavement long before mine, and that I would grope through weeds and falling tombstones in the Enfield churchyard, the muffled roar of North London traffic muted by crowding yews, as I searched for a stone which might mark the place where they put her body, beside Charles who had died 13 long years earlier, and near the boy named William (who had once delighted the ladies of the court in Cochin China) and the infant William who had hardly lived at all.

The information I needed for my petroglyph-ship article was not in the *Reminiscences* and I returned the notebook to the librarian but Frances Barkley's path had crossed mine, and she began to nag me. Soon I found myself back in the archives, reading the other letters and documents in the Barkley files, the article by Captain Walbran entitled "The Cruise of the *Imperial Eagle*," and the discussion of the mystery of the missing Diary of Frances Barkley by W. Kaye Lamb in the *British Columbia Historical Journal*. I was surprised that I had read so little of the Barkley story elsewhere, and I began to realize that their fur-trading competitor Captain Meares had not only succeeded in stealing the Barkley discoveries but had also supplanted

Captain Barkley in the history books. Frances lashed out in anger against him in her *Reminiscences,* but her words were buried in that thin notebook locked in the vaults of the archives. Possibly her *Reminiscences* should be published, I thought. The shape of a book began to form.

The first task was to find the present owners of the *Reminiscences* and discover whether they wished them published, and whether any other letters or documents existed, to fill in, if possible, the many blank years of the *Reminiscences.* There was no hope of finding Frances Barkley's Diary, for this document, a sea journal written at the time of the voyages, had almost certainly been burned in a house fire at Westholme, Vancouver Island, in 1909. Fortunately, Frances had used her Diary as a source in writing her *Reminiscences* and Captain Walbran also used the Diary in writing a published account of the *Imperial Eagle.* As the Diary had been burned on Vancouver Island, I began the search for the Barkley descendants there. An account of how I found Commander Barnes, the owner of the *Reminiscences,* and the many other descendants in England, is not relevant here, although the documents which were examined and photographed have added many details to the Barkley story. I am very grateful to all the Barkley descendants, whose interest and encouragement and assistance would have delighted Frances and Charles. For her invaluable aid in the search for those modern Barkleys, I am also much indebted to Margaret Knight of Cambridge, a friend who gave me many hours of her time.

In the quest for Frances Barkley in England, one strange synchronistic event seems worth relating here. It occurred at Whitminster House in the Vale of Berkeley, at one of the first of our Barkley interviews. When we arrived for lunch, we were greeted by our host and hostess with the information that Miss Violet Barlow, an old friend of Louise (Barkley) Teesdale who had died in 1952, had arrived unexpectedly, just a few moments ahead of us, and that she would of course be a member of the luncheon party. Miss Barlow had not been at Whitminster House for many years, but chance had brought her there for the precise two hours of our visit. When we were presented to her and our mission explained, she sat up very straight and announced that she knew all about Frances Barkley because she had read her Diary in 1934, and in the very drawing room in which we sipped sherry that day. I immediately concluded that Miss Barlow had read a copy of the *Reminiscences,* but she went on to tell a dramatic story she recalled from the Diary, a story which was not in the *Reminiscences*. It would seem that Miss Barlow had appeared out of the blue to tell me that the Diary had not been burned at Westholme.

Subsequent discoveries that summer confirmed that the Diary almost certainly existed until about 1952, but there the trail vanished. Although I have not given up hope of finding it, it seemed sensible to proceed with the project of publishing the *Reminiscences*, including all the new data uncovered in the search. Perhaps the publication of this book and new interest in the Barkleys will lead to the discovery of the missing Diary.

Beth Hill

Preface to the Second Edition

With the publication of this second edition of *The Remarkable World of Frances Barkley*, it was decided to revisit Frances' journey in the hope that her Diary had been found. It has been 25 years since the first printing of this book and ample time for the Diary to appear from the dust swirls of an attic, basement or sea-chest. Unfortunately, the missing journal has not turned up so one has to assume, at this point, that the Diary is lost.

This second edition maintains the wonderful story and writings as Beth Hill first composed them. There is some reorganization of the material and additional information about the maritime sea trade, the power of the East India Company, and the challenge of a seafaring life for women as well as expanded descriptions of some people, events and places.

Frances' experiences still reach out and her *Reminiscences* weave a magical tale for her audience 200 years after she first set foot aboard the *Imperial Eagle*. Her story is one of high adventure, love, betrayal, money, death and loyalty and, above all, it offers up a shining piece of the mosaic of world history.

Cathy Converse

Introduction

*F*rances Trevor was born in the same year as both Wellington and Napoleon, 1769, but she mentioned neither of these famous men in her *Reminiscences*. Like a fish in the sea, she was carried relentlessly by the great tides of history, unaware of the forces which controlled her movements, for her lifespan witnessed the violent birth of the modern age. Under the cool Palladian surface of the Classical world of country squires, Tom Jones, "Farmer George" III, mansions designed by Wren, a largely rural and fairly static time of ranked society and immemorial traditions, the forces of change were boiling, and would erupt, during Frances' lifetime, in the American and French revolutions. The first steam engine was sputtering just four years before she was born, and the whirring of the earliest spinning machine accompanied her arrival. The clever English scientists were optimistically assembling that clanking machine, the Industrial Revolution, which, like Frankenstein's Monster, would turn on its creators and henceforth control the lives of all. It is not easy for the person of today to know what it was like to be alive during Frances' lifetime. Telstar and television are little help in looking backward into an age when time moved with the slow pace of sun and season and was not measured into working days and hours; before Mr. Wedgewood had invented "clocking in"; before man became a cog in a machine. Men who fly round the rim of Earth inside a silver bullet, concerned as to the rareness of microwave-cooked steak, achieving in a few hours the journey which took a year in the lives of Frances and Charles Barkley, may find it difficult to understand the quality of life 200 years ago.

The Barkleys looked upon an England which was far lovelier, with millions of acres of unspoilt woodland, great rolling heaths purple with heather and yellow with the dying bracken. There were birds then which are no longer seen — the golden oriole and the rose-coloured pastor, the eagle and the great bustard. When Frances was young there was much more land unenclosed: the meadow lands along the rivers where hay was grown, ploughlands for growing the village crops, divided into strips and scraps of land by boundaries of coarse grass, where wheat, barley, rye and oats were grown. Wheat was for export and for the bread of the upper classes, barley was for the brewers and the poor man's bread, and oats were for the horses. As the population increased, from 5,000,000 at the beginning of the 18th century to about 9,000,000 toward its close, the old inefficient agricultural methods were not adequate. Land was enclosed (i.e., taken over by the powerful families and fenced into large fields which could then produce a saleable surplus for the owner) and more food was grown; however, as wheat could be profitably exported, the poor went hungry, being driven off the land which had once fed them. They were forced to live in the expanding cities where they served as cheap labour for the new machines, and around the factory cities the countryside turned black as the new mills polluted the rivers and shrouded the land in smoke.

To run factories effectively, a new code of industrial discipline had to be invented, with new work habits, diligence and long hours. The required transformation in social attitudes may be compared to the change Westerners have forced upon the First Nations people Frances regarded as savages. R. Cookson, a hosier, appearing before the Committee on the Woollen Manufacture of England in 1866 is recorded in the Parliamentary Papers making this complaint about the work habits of the men of Frances' time:

> I found the utmost distaste, on the part of the men, to any regular hours or regular habits ... The men themselves were considerably dissatisfied because they could not go in and out as they pleased and have what holidays they pleased, and go on just as they had been used to do.[1]

This is a degree of freedom that people of today cannot even imagine. Nor can those, accustomed to hourly news reports from every part of the shrinking globe, easily envisage living upon an Earth as unknown and mysterious as it was 200 years ago. Romantic and exciting accounts written by courageous explorers like the Barkleys, when tiny vessels ventured across vast seas to visit exotic peoples tantalize the spirit of adventure. As the fabulous wealth of this distant world was revealed, the greedy Europeans reached out to grasp it.

When Charles William Barkley was born in 1759, Robert Clive was laying the foundations in India for British exploitation of that marvellous and incredibly wealthy land, and the Battle of Quebec was being fought to secure Britain's hold on the furs and forests of North America. There was wealth to be won everywhere. Through Frances' lifetime, intermittent wars went on as the European powers fought like snarling dogs over meaty bones. From 1783 to 1815 there were 22 years of war and only 10 of peace, but it was during those few years of peace that most of the sea adventures of Frances and Charles took place.

In England there was a genuine moral fervour for a policy of commercial imperialism; England's grandeur was the will of God, and war was virtuous as well as necessary, and would be rewarded with victories, wealth and power. Such a policy led to war, and war with France (the Seven Years' War) broke out in earnest in 1756. Prime Minister William Pitt fought it by destroying not the French Empire, but French trade, by blockading the French fleet in Brest and Toulon. Trade was wealth and power, and Frances and Charles lived their lives in this world of expanding trade and ruthless competition for new wealth. The hapless sea otter of the northwest coast was part of this new wealth.

When Frances was first brought to Ormond Street in London at the age of five, she was too young to observe the lively city, growing at an unprecedented rate. There was a ferment of talk in the new coffee houses. People argued such questions as whether political liberty could be achieved without the introduction of the ballot box. Between 1753 and 1792 the number of newspapers doubled, a product of and a factor in the new political awareness. Everyone talked about the trouble in the American colonies. Should the Americans be taxed to help pay the costs of the defence of the new colony? The majority of English politicians were inflexible on the theoretical relationship between England and her colonies: colonies were ordained by God to provide raw materials and to accept manufactured articles in return, and all trade must be carried in British ships — the mercantilist faith was fairly simple. However, new ideas as to the rights of the common man were rumbling and giving warnings of eruptions to come, in America and in France and everywhere.

England had captured her possessions in North America in the Seven Years' War, which ended in 1763, six years before Frances was born; British victories had also opened Europe to British trade and subsequently enabled the Reverend Dr. John Trevor, Frances Barkley's father, to move his family to Hamburg. While Frances was growing up in Germany, the American Revolution began, and General Washington turned his farmers and backwoodsmen into the disciplined army which defeated the British redcoats and the Prussians. At sea, American ships became privateers and preyed on the British merchant ships. In 1778 the French joined the war against England, and the Spaniards and Dutch took the opportunity to strike a blow against their most aggressive trade adversary, Great Britain. In India, where young Charles had already gone to sea on the East India Company ships, a formidable combination of Indian rulers, backed by the French, threatened British power. The news being circulated in London's coffee houses was bleak indeed. However, at the Battle of the Saintes in April of 1782, a brilliant British victory over the combined Franco-Spanish fleets in the West Indies helped to strengthen Britain's hand in the negotiations for peace, and the Peace of Versailles in 1783 gave freedom to the American colonies and a respite from the wars.

In the same year as the Versailles settlement, the Reverend Dr. Trevor was undertaking his new duties in Ostend and his daughter Frances was entering a French convent to be educated. In England George Augustus Frederic was made prince regent. The world seemed peaceful, most of its people deaf to the rumblings of change, unaware that in six years the fall of the Bastille would signal the eruption of the French Revolution.

In those ten years of comparative calm, between the Peace of Versailles and the beginning of the long Napoleonic Wars, Frances Trevor and Charles Barkley met in Ostend, fell in love and made their long voyage around the world, which Frances recorded in her Diary and wrote about in the *Reminiscences* published here.

Through the eyes of Frances Hornby Trevor Barkley the world of the late 18th century may be surveyed. The life of this well-travelled and observant woman tied together the places and events at the height of the British maritime trade. To share the wind-blown voyages of the *Imperial Eagle* and the *Halcyon* is to bear witness to the beginning of a new chapter in the history and discovery of the northwest coast of North America. For thousands of years this coast was home to the Nuu-chah-nulth, the Coast Salish, the Kwakwak'wakw, the Nuxalk, the Heiltsuk, and the Tlingit, among others. This demographic was severely altered with the appearance at Nootka Sound of Spanish and British explorers, and the merchant fur traders who followed. The 40 years of the maritime fur trade, spanning the time from 1788 to 1825, contain the story of upheaval and cultural shifts of the coastal peoples whose territorial waters were transgressed, as well as the intensive pursuit and eventual extinction of the sea otter. Frances' writings offer a first-hand account of how and why this fog-shrouded place of drowned mountains was, briefly, of great interest in the high courts of the world.

Life on the sailing ships has frequently been romanticized in film and fiction, but the reality was harsh — the tedium, the sickening diet, the stench, the stresses resulting from imprisoning a small group of people in cramped quarters for uncertain lengths of time. Dr. Johnson remarked in 1759 that "No man will be a sailor who has continence to get himself into jail, for being in a ship is being in jail with the chance of being drowned. A man in jail has more room, better food and commonly better company."[2]

In such conditions, illness was hard to avoid. Captain Barkley was seriously ill on both voyages, and Frances was to lose one child at sea, the victim of a tropical fever. Typhus and dysentery were the shore diseases of Europe, and in the tropics the seamen got malaria, yellow fever, hookworm and typhus. Lice and fleas were taken for granted, and the lice carried typhus. Venereal diseases were considered an occupational ailment of sailors and in the 18th century, treatment was ineffective. In port the sailors were frequently not allowed ashore for fear of desertions, but boatloads of prostitutes were ferried to the ship; the scene below decks can be imagined and it is not surprising that syphilis and gonorrhea were widespread.

There were also the natural hazards: uncharted rocks, ice, lightning, waterspouts, monsoons and terrible hurricanes. Strong winds could be dangerous but so were the doldrums, when the sails flapped uselessly and the ship rolled in the swell and tensions increased as the days dragged past. Morale was of overwhelming importance in long voyages, and any Pacific voyage was long indeed. To all this must be added the threat of attack from pirates or privateers, or from other European ships during the intermittent wars, and the danger of being killed by native peoples; the Barkleys lost six men, killed by natives on the coast of North America.

Into this world stepped Frances Barkley. She may have been the first woman to circumnavigate the world; this honour is also claimed for Jeanne Baret, a Frenchwoman who sailed with Bougainville's expedition in 1763, disguised as the valet of Commerson, a scientist on the voyage. The earliest women at sea were probably stowaways also. Just as the institution of "camp follower" is as old as the armies they accompanied, so it is reasonable to suspect that the stowaway female is as old as ships large enough to hide her. If her protector was of sufficiently high rank, she walked openly upon the decks. There are, of course, few records concerning stowaway women, but in 1589 printed orders to the Spanish captains of the vessels of the Armada explicitly prohibited women on board and threatened severe punishment for anyone disobeying the order, clear evidence that the custom of hiding women below decks was an ancient one. Like the rats which shared the stinking hold where she would hide, furtiveness was the passport of the stowaway woman. Sometimes these shadowy figures were only seen when they were dead. In 1636, when the *Anne Royal* was lying on her side in the mud, part of her keel broken off, the report included the words "Divers men drowned, and some women."

Not until 1731 do we find official admission in the British navy of this matter, tacitly ignored. In that year an Admiralty publication, under "Instructions to the Captain," stated "He is not to carry any woman to sea ... without Orders from the Admiralty,"[3] and in 1756 the orders were more detailed: "That no Woman ever be permitted on Board, but such as are really the Wives of the Men they come to, and the Ship not to be too much pestered even with them."[4] The word "really" makes this order difficult to enforce. How little it was obeyed is shown by the fact that there were women, Ann Hopping and Mary Anne Riley, who applied for the medals being awarded after the Battle of the Nile in 1798; they were refused, for the strange reason that "many women in the fleet were equally useful."[5] It is a sad comment on the times that the stowaway women went into the horror of the holds to endure near-starvation, wormy biscuits, live rats, storms, cold and misery because their lives on shore were so wretched that such a life on board ship was preferable. Sometimes the sailors' wives came because their husbands were so poorly and infrequently paid that they would have starved if left behind.

It was not until about 1850, after Frances Barkley's time, that new ship designs, new standards of cleanliness, better pay for sailors, the provision of regular shore-leaves and above all, higher standards of living for both ship and shore made the stowaway women a secret of the past. Given the evidence for hidden women, it seems unwise to state who was the first woman to circumnavigate the world, but perhaps Frances can claim to be the first non-stowaway woman to round Cape Horn, reach Hawaii, and arrive on the British Columbia and Alaska coasts.

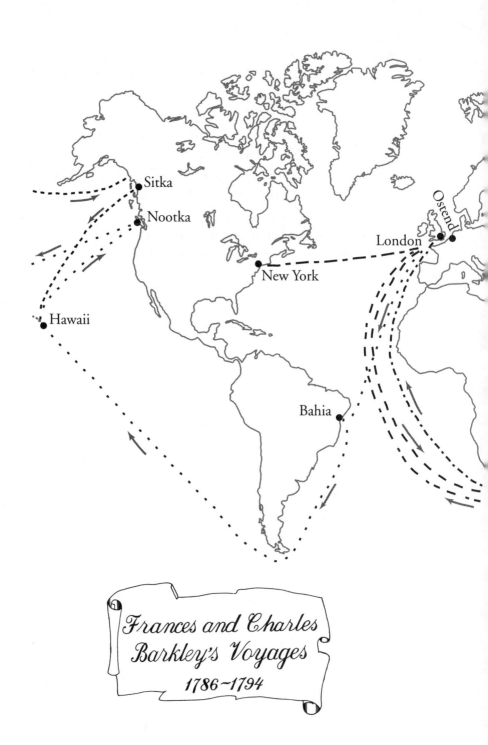

Frances and Charles Barkley's Voyages 1786~1794

St. Peter and
St. Paul

Canton
Macao
Cochin
China

Calcutta

Bombay

Madras

Mauritius

Legend

"Imperial Eagle"(Loudoun) ~ Nov. 1786 – 1788
- - - - - - - Ostend to Mauritius

American vessel ~ Nov. 1789
- - · - · - · Mauritius to England

"Princess Frederica" ~ May 1791 – Aug. 1791
- - - - - England to Calcutta

"Halcyon" ~ Dec. 1791 – June 1793
- - - - - - Calcutta – Alaska – Mauritius

"Betsy" ~ 1793 – 1794
- - — - - Mauritius to England

"Amphion" ~ Nov. 1794
- - - - - New York to England

Chapter One
The Trevors and the Barkleys

ines looped across a map of the world show the voyages of Frances and Charles Barkley, made between 1786 and 1794. Frances was only 17 years old and a bride when she began the travels in which she circumnavigated the world and was the first English-woman to visit Hawaii, British Columbia and Alaska.

As merchant sea traders the Barkleys followed the route of the newly established sea-otter trade that was opened up by Captain James Cook in 1778. Carrying copper, iron and brass from Europe, mariners hoped to take advantage of the lucrative trade in sea-otter pelts along the northwest coast of the Pacific. The soft, exquisite fur of the sea otter, known as "soft gold" in the trade, was greatly desired by the wealthy mandarins of China. They would pay dearly for the opportunity to adorn their clothing with the red-rusty-brown pelt of the *Enhydra lutris*; it was utterly irresistible and added greatly to their status as a signal of wealth and importance. From the northwest coast the merchant traders would set out across the Pacific Ocean, taking advantage of the favourable trade winds and the north equatorial current for the 7,560-nautical mile (14,000-kilometre) trip to Macao. In China they would exchange their cargo for tea, silks and porcelain to take back to Europe. Such a venture was a huge undertaking and it would sometimes take four or five years, with the wind, currents and weather often determining a ship's course. According to Judge F. W. Howay, an international authority on the maritime fur trade, the ordinary cargo of a northwest trader ranged in value between $20,000 and $30,000, yet some carried cargoes up to $450,000. Marine underwriters do not make money out of losses. The merchant fur trade was an expensive undertaking and the foggy, uncharted waters of the northwest coast added enormous risk which only the wealthiest or most daring were willing to take on. The value of an investment averaged approximately £120,000 ($514,285) per annum with no guarantees.[1] In addition to brokers, backers and insurers, the ship's master usually made a heavy investment in the voyage with the possibility of spending years at sea for little remuneration or none at all. Captain Barkley addressed the debt and expenses incurred by the master in a letter he wrote to his brother John, undated but possibly in 1809:

> Let us now look at the Remuneration; If the Ship sells all her
> Cargoe and returns safe, the Captain gets a £1000; this will cost for
> Insurance 30 per Ct., 305 £ to cover prem., 95 £ makes £410,
> leaves £590 for the voyages. If she sells only half her Cargoe, the
> Insurance is the same & the Captn. will get only £90, let the voyage
> be ever so long. Several ships have out, viz. the *Antelope* near two
> years, the *Higginston* 18 Mos. & in May last had not sold for three
> thousand pounds. But suppose she returns only selling a third, then
> he loses £200 & all his wages will not pay his Insurance.[2]

It is difficult to estimate just how many masters made their fortunes in the private trade but there is evidence that some did fairly well. The Barkleys did not fare so well because of inauspicious events beyond their control.

Frances and Charles Barkley made two fur-trading expeditions to the Northwest Coast of North America. The first, from 1786 to 1788, in the ship *Loudoun*, renamed the *Imperial Eagle* and flying Austrian colours, took them from Ostend to Brazil, around the Horn to Hawaii, and then to Nootka Sound on the west coast of Vancouver Island. Trading with the coastal people for the skins of the sea otter, the Barkleys sailed southwards along the Vancouver Island shore, discovering and naming Barkley Sound and rediscovering the Strait of Juan de Fuca, which Captain Cook had missed nine years earlier. They then sailed to China and sold the pelts in Canton receiving 30,000 Spanish dollars for their cargo of 800 pelts. Barkley had intended sailing on to Calcutta where he was expecting to make a second trip to the northwest coast; however, while in Mauritius he was unjustly relieved of command of the *Imperial Eagle* by his agents. After having made £10,000 for their backers, the Barkleys returned to England, angry at the injustice of the event, incensed at the temerity of the agents and feeling defrauded from the loss of their investment of time and money.

In May 1791, the Barkleys set sail again, joining the huge fleet of ships trading between Europe and Bombay. This time Captain Barkley was in command of the 1,200-ton *Princess Frederica*, carrying British trade goods and passengers to India. It was their intention to settle in Calcutta and conduct coastal trade. Their venture would probably have proved successful and given the Barkleys a comfortable life had their plans not been upset by Charles' older brother. It seems that Captain John Barkley, himself an East India Company employee, felt that the life of a merchant mariner was a more suitable calling for his brother. The Barkleys were ships' masters, an honourable and coveted position, and to do less was to be less.

Charles and Frances reluctantly set out on a second fur-trading endeavour to the Pacific northwest coast. Charles purchased and outfitted two vessels — the 80-ton brig *Halcyon* and the still-smaller *Venus* — and they sailed northward in search of the sea otter. The Barkleys spent many weeks at St. Peter and St. Paul, a village in Siberian Kamchatka, where the Russian officials frustrated their attempts to trade. Sailing east across the North Pacific, they reached the Alaskan coast, where they traded for furs with the Tlingit people until the oncoming winter and a shortage of provisions led them to sail to Hawaii, to meet the *Venus*. Failing to rendezvous with their partner vessel, the *Halcyon* proceeded to Canton, and after the furs had been traded, the Barkleys visited Cochin China before sailing to Mauritius to sell the cargo, probably tea, purchased in Canton. Upon their arrival at that French island, they were surprised to discover that France and England were at war again, their ship was a prize and themselves prisoners. Through the influence of French friends they were allowed to depart on an American vessel to the newly independent United States, where they bought the vessel *Amphion*, loaded it with American goods and sailed it to England, completing their second voyage and Frances' adventures at sea.

Thus the eight years of the voyages of Charles and Frances Barkley can be briefly summarized. Their exploits have had little attention from historians, partly because Charles Barkley published no account of them and partly because the slippery Captain John Meares acquired Barkley's charts from the owner of the *Imperial Eagle* and subsequently published a book about his own voyages, taking credit for discoveries made by Barkley and others. It is possible that anger over the neglect of her husband's achievements moved Frances Barkley, at the age of 66, to write the *Reminiscences*, published here for the first time. After beginning to write, and finding her memory unequal to the task, she apparently searched among old papers and found the notes she had written at the time of the voyages. This incomplete sea journal is the Diary which has been the subject of some controversy among historians. Although Frances used the Diary as a sourcebook in writing the *Reminiscences*, she did not transfer all the information, and in fact failed to ever complete the *Reminiscences*. It has therefore been necessary to compile the Barkley story from a number of sources, detailed in the Notes on the Sources.

It is hard to imagine Frances' feelings, and her writings are largely silent on such things. What was it like for this young woman, barely 17 years of age, to leave behind everything she knew and take up residence aboard a ship, to travel to places unknown and suffer danger, pain, heartbreak, extreme privation and war, in addition to all the hazards of the sea. And all this without the loving support of her family or friends.

When she was young, her long, red-gold hair was unbelievably lovely. Her children's children's children told of her "unpinning a shower of golden hair" and releasing "a cloud of hair to her feet." The people of Nootka Sound had worshipped her as a goddess, South Seas islanders thought her divine, and her wondrous hair played to her release by pirates, they would say. In one accounting by her great-granddaughter the following story was related:

> a curious and what was nearly a disastrous episode, but was luckily averted owing to Mrs. Barkley's wonderful hair. She was celebrated for the enormous mass of beautiful golden hair which when down was so thick and long as to ressemble a thick cloak. While coasting down the Chinese coast, they were boarded and taken prisoners by the Chinese and she and her little boy and her husband were taken ashore, where they sat down with the child in much alarm as to what their captors would do to them. The Chinese women crowded around, never having seen such a fair white skinned woman before and started pulling out her hair pins, whereupon her wonderful hair

fell down to the ground covering her as with a golden mantle. This so amazed the natives that, believing she was not an ordinary mortal being, they hurried them back to their ship and let them depart![3]

There are two other versions of this incident. According to one great-great-grandson, when the *Imperial Eagle* was anchored off Nootka, the Indians on board became dangerously aggressive, but suddenly Frances emerged from the cabin with her hair hanging free, like a golden cloud, and the Indians fell down before her, thinking she was a goddess. Another family line preserves a legend of Frances and Charles, ashore upon a South Seas island for water, being suddenly captured by natives who emerged from the forest. Charles and the other crew members were tied up, and feared for their lives. Again, it was the curious women who loosed Frances' hair, which fell like a shower of gold, and so amazed the natives that they thought her divine. Frances ordered Captain Barkley and the crew released and then indicated that the water butts should be filled, and they all

Constance, Lady Parker of Waddington, a great-granddaughter of Frances Barkley. Constance Parker is said to have closely resembled Frances.

departed safely from the island. It is not known whether any true incident lies behind the legends, but no such tales appear in the *Reminiscences*.

But in 1836 her hair was grey and pinned behind her head. Frances Barkley was old. Charles had been buried at Enfield three years earlier, and after his death she had given up her fine house at Hertford and had lived quietly at Clapton, busy with the affairs of children and grandchildren. As her life narrowed toward its end, she looked back as through a telescope, enlarging the high times when she was young, when she and Charles had sailed the strange new world Cook had discovered. Meares and Cook and the others had published their accounts of their voyages, but Charles lay dead and forgotten. The young people knew little of his great achievements and courage, and would remember less, and even for Frances the memories were fading. Forgetting even that she had once written some notes in a sea journal 50 years earlier, she decided to write her *Reminiscences*. She purchased a small notebook with a pretty, oiled-water cover and began her task:[4]

> May 2d in the Year 1836
> The following Narrative of my Voyages and Adventures of my life, Penned by me in the 66th year of my Age, must be considered in the light of a Reminiscence of former days, not a correct tradition, being founded on very vague Data, as I never kept any Journal. It might, however, be improved by refferance to Logbooks & Sea journals, if I had courage to Peruse them, but it is too late in the day for such a reserch. To begin then:
> I was born at Bridgewater in Somersetshire. My Father, the Revd Doctor Trevor was Rector of Otterhampton, where I was christened in the Year 1772, being then upwards of two years old. My Mother, whose name was Beacher, died when I was an Infant and a Twin, by all account a very weakly child. My Father Married a second Wife, Miss Harriot Smith of Bridgewater, he having by my Mother living at that time four Daughters, Harriot James, now Mrs. Cook, Jane Rebecca, now Mrs. Mullens, My Twin sister Elizabeth who died at Hambourgh in her seventh year, and myself Frances, all the three survivers being Widows. My Father had four sons by his second Wife, John, Frederic, Charles and Henry, three of whom are now living, Married and have numerous Families, excepting Fredc. who is a Bachilor. It would be tedious for me to follow up the various peregrinations of our Childhood. My Father, being an expensive man, contrived to spend a handsome Fortune & being of a restless disposition, a few years after his second Marriage, quitted Bridgewater and came up to London and took a

A view of Bridgwater, Somerset, showing the spire of St. Mary's Church. Painted by John Chubb, in 1796.

House in Ormond Street. The journey, arrival at Bath, and the second day in London, is the first thing I recollect, at which time I must have been about five years old. As all the Boys but John & Fredc. were Born at Hamburg, where my Father took his Family when the latter was an Infant; indeed I believe he was born at Hamburg as well as the other two.

We went from England to Roterdam, and the story goes that I was put into a Birth on board the Traeder on which we were boarded, and that I slept very comfortably the whole Passage, whilst My Father, Mother in Law, three sisters, the Infant and two Maidservants were all dreadfully afflicted with sea sickness. So that it seems I was destined to make a good sailor. From Roterdam we proceeded in two Carraiges, called Post Coaches, which my Father bought for the journey to Hamburg. For particulars, see My Fathers Journal.

At this point in her narrative, Frances left nine blank pages, and when she began again she wrote of her marriage to Captain Charles William Barkley. What do those empty pages omit? Did she find it difficult to write about the restless, rich and mysterious John Trevor, her father, "an expensive man," as she comments caustically? Why does she not write of her origins, in an age when birth and breeding were of paramount importance? Possibly Frances decided to consult her sister Harriot Cook, almost ten years older than herself. However, the blank pages remained, and nothing is known to this day concerning John Trevor's Journal.

One possible explanation for the empty pages has been found. Constance, Lady Parker of Waddington, a great-granddaughter of Frances Barkley, wrote:

Ormond Street, London. Drawn by J. F. Whittingham.

The Rev. John Trevor was the son of Lord Hampden by a first marriage. The proofs of this marriage which took place at the Fleet Prison were in the possession of his daughter Harriot Cook. She destroyed them for the sake of her son, receiving for them large hush moneys from her uncle, who succeeded to the title instead of her father.[5]

Fleet Prison is certainly not an appropriate place for the marriage of Lord Hampden. A genealogical chart owned by another Barkley descendant plainly shows John Trevor descended from the great John Hampden, a famous parliamentarian and principal leader of the Long Parliament in its opposition to Charles I, and before that from Cromwell's grandfather. John Trevor married a woman of whom nothing is known except her name; possibly this marriage was against his family's wishes and was the reason he was deprived of his inheritance.

Some pages survive of an account written in 1913 by Henry Edward Trevor, barrister-at-law, who conducted extensive research without uncovering the secret hidden in the missing journal of John Trevor. He does tell us that his great-grandfather John Trevor was born August 13, 1740, and that he was married when very young to a certain Jane Beacher. A daughter, Harriot, was born shortly thereafter, and when the Trevors were living in Castle Street in Canterbury,[6] in 1766, a second daughter, Jane Rebecca, was born. In 1769 two more daughters arrived, twins, Elizabeth and Frances. By the time of the birth of the twin girls, John and Jane Trevor were living in Bridgwater, Somerset. Frances wrote that she was christened at Otterhampton in 1772, but an ancient register in the vaults of St. Mary's Church in Bridgwater records in fading ink that Elizabeth and Frances, daughters of John and Jane Trevor, were christened April 6, 1769, the same year as their birth.

Two years later John Trevor was ordained priest at Wells in the bishop's private chapel, and on the following day, with what his great-grandson described as "amazing dispatch" he was admitted to the rectory of Otterhampton on the presentation of Mr. John Evered the Younger, of Bridgwater. Seven miles west of Bridgwater, the tiny church still stands beside a lane where wildflowers grow. Otterhampton provided John Trevor with a living of less than £50 per year. There was no parsonage and probably the Trevor family continued to live in Bridgwater. Possibly Jane Trevor was ill, for only four months later, the pen of the new vicar recorded in his parish register the death of his own wife: "Jane, wife of the Rev. John Trevor, Rector of this parish, was buried in the chancel, October 13, 1771." This is Jane Beacher's only memorial; no carved stone or gleaming brass marks the place were Frances Barkley's mother was buried.

Another two years elapsed before the four girls acquired a stepmother. John Trevor married Harriot Smith, the daughter of the Bridgwater Collector of Customs, and in this second marriage four sons were born. The first, John William, arrived in 1774, just before the move to London, and is the infant dreadfully afflicted with seasickness on the passage to Rotterdam the

John Trevor, father of Frances Barkley.

following year. In 1775 the family witnessed the birth of a second son, Frederic John, who died in infancy, a sad year which also saw the death of Frances' twin sister, Elizabeth. Another Frederic was born in 1776 in Hamburg (the year the American colonists declared independence) when Frances was seven. This was also the year in which the Reverend Dr. John Trevor became chaplain to the Earl of Deloraine.

The Scottish title Earl of Deloraine was created for Henry Scott in 1676. The fourth, and last, Earl of Deloraine was a Henry Scott born in 1737, three years before his chaplain, John Trevor. It is recorded that in the early part of his life he was "extremely conspicuous"[7] in the English circles of fashion where he dissipated a fine estate. In middle age he "secured from the wreck of his fortune an annuity of £1000 per annum on which he lived afterwards very privately."[8] Married in 1763, he had no children and the marriage was not a happy one. His wife Frances separated from him and withdrew to a convent in France where she died in 1782. It would seem that Henry Scott and John Trevor had much in common, and may well have been old friends.

It is not known why John Trevor journeyed from London to Rotterdam in 1775, but upon his arrival, with his entire family, he furnished a house as if for a long stay; however, after a journey to The Hague, he purchased two post coaches and transferred himself, his wife, the four girls and the infant John to Hamburg, the furniture following by sea. In Hamburg he held the post of chaplain to the English community until 1780, and during these years Frederic, Charles and Henry were born. In 1783 John Trevor was appointed the first minister of the newly established Protestant Chapel at Ostend; at the founding meeting of this church, he is described as Rector of Otterhampton and chaplain to Henry, Earl of Deloraine, so it is apparent that he continued to hold these two offices. The new chapel was established so that the British Protestant inhabitants of Ostend could enjoy the rights accorded them under the terms of several Imperial edicts which permitted Protestant subjects to exercise their religion in any place where one hundred or more such families were settled; this privilege was swept away in the Napoleonic Wars of 1803-1815. With John Trevor's move from Hamburg to Ostend, his family was broken up; his wife Harriot with her four sons returned to Bridgwater and apparently never rejoined her husband. Two of the daughters are supposed to have found homes with her relatives, but Harriot, aged 20 at this time, was soon married to James Cook. Jane Rebecca, seven years younger than Harriot, was not married until 1787, when His Grace the Archbishop gave a special licence to allow her to be married in Canterbury Cathedral to John Mullens of Portsmouth. Thus Jane returned for her marriage to the city where she had been born 21 years earlier. The Reverend Dr. John Trevor gave the bride away, and after this event we know nothing of him except the date of his death, aged 54, in 1794. Not even the place where he lies buried has been recorded.

What happened to Frances when the family dissolved? It is known that she was educated at a convent on the continent, and the retreat of Frances Scott, the wife of John Trevor's friend and patron, the Earl of Deloraine, to a French convent may be relevant here. The account of Frances Hornby Trevor Barkley recorded by her great-granddaughter Constance Parker states:

> She was educated at a Roman Catholic Convent and besides the usual subjects was also taught sewing, embroidery, cooking, domestic housework and distilling. She was a brilliant French scholar and her knowledge of French and French habits and customs were of

great use to her later on. She left the Convent when seventeen years old.[9]

Thus it happened that in 1786 Frances Trevor, with the long red-gold hair, was with her father in Ostend when young Captain Barkley sailed into that port in the fine ship *Loudoun*.

> I was Married to my late Lamented Husband Charles Win.
> Barkley Esqr. on the 17th October 1786, he being in his 26th
> year, and I in my 17th. We were Married in the Protastant
> Chapel at Ostend in Flanders, of which my Father was Minister,
> by whom the Maraige Ceremony was performed in the presence
> of several Friends, several of whom subscribed their Names in
> the Register of the Chapel as follow,

Planning to make a search for the marriage document, Frances left an inch and a half blank so that she could fill in the names later, then wrote:

> Charles William Barkley was brought up in the Honourable
> East India Company's sea service ...

From "Remarks moored at Ostend" in the back of the logbook, it is known that the courtship could not have been longer than six weeks, but Frances writes nothing about this time, nor about the wedding and the preparations for their departure on a voyage which might last 10 years. She does not even write much about Charles.

A brief courtship and a quick proposal were not unusual for someone in the merchant service; times in port were always short and there was never any certainty about when the ship would return. Frances married her captain with all due British propriety. While it is not known precisely what Frances' bridal gown looked like, in all probability she would have chosen a dress that could be worn at a later time. Women's dresses were too expensive and difficult to obtain to have a one-event garment. Shopping wisely and wanting something special to mark the event Frances could have walked down the aisle wearing a gown of wool or blue damask with a white or crimson insert on the front. Elbow-length sleeves and falling cuffs would be offset by folds of pleats adorning the back of her gown. Frances' golden hair curled and, dropped to its length, would have been crowned by a large hat, tipped smartly up on one side. Her groom would have been appropriately attired in his officers' dress uniform, wearing his gold-braided navy jacket as befitting a man of his stature.

The name Frances acquired with her young captain was old and distinguished. It could be traced to the Norman Berchelais, who came to England with William the Conqueror and who built Berkely Castle near the Severn Estuary in southwest England. A member of this family, John Berkeley, rode to Scotland in 1068 in the train of Margaret, sister of King Edgar Atheling. Margaret journeyed north to marry Scotland's King Malcolm Canmore, who subsequently gave John Berkeley the lands of Towie in Aberdeen. Descending from the Barkleys of Towie, there was a James Barkley, of Himglende near Cromarty, on the wild northeast coast of Scotland. It is said that the family did well by smuggling, but Constance Parker's account is perhaps more accurate:

> Many younger sons in those days invested their monies in
> sailing vessels and some cargo like spices, tea or furs … which on
> being brought home would be sold to dealers who often paid
> badly but sufficiently to enable a refit and start again on fresh
> adventures.[10]

In the depressed years after the terrible defeat of Bonnie Prince Charles at Culloden in 1746, when the Highlands were poverty-stricken and closely watched by English revenue officers, and there was money for neither smuggling nor trade, the three sons of James Barkley were forced to leave Scotland to seek their fortunes in the wide world. The youngest, Charles (father of Frances Trevor's husband, Captain Charles William Barkley), went to sea in the service of the East India Company, becoming the captain of the Indiaman *Pacific*. He married a woman named Martha, of whom it is known only that she was renounced in her husband's will of 1776, the same year he drowned in the Hooghly River near Calcutta. They had three children: John, whom Frances was to call her "evil star," was born in 1748; Martha, named after her mother, arrived 10 years later, and in the next year, 1759, Charles William was born. Sister Martha, who had two marriages, the first husband having the surname Budgen and the second Hornby, maintained close ties with John's family, and is buried beside them in Enfield.

Ten years before Charles Barkley's death by drowning, a letter from the East India Company director at Fort William (Calcutta) to the directors in London gives a glimpse of the captain of the *Pacific*:

> The writers of last season appointed to this establishment are arrived and have been stationed to different offices except Mr. Faugoing, who died in the passage, and Mr. George Bright, supposed to be on the *Hector* or *Falmouth*.
>
> Conformable to your repeated orders we called the writers before us on their arrival and questioned them concerning the treatment they met with on their passage, who declared themselves satisfied with the behavior of the different commanders; in justice, however, to Captain Barkley we cannot omit mentioning that the gentlemen who came on board the *Pacifick* expressed in very particular terms their satisfaction at the attention and civilities he shewed them.[11]

It would seem that young Captain Charles William Barkley resembled his father, for Frances' *Reminiscences* tell of many parties and dinners on board the ships, and she speaks of Charles William as a man of exuberant spirits, fond of company and show.

In 1770, only six years before his father's death, 11-year-old Charles William went aboard the *Pacific* to begin his naval training. His older brother John, 11 years his senior, was already at sea. A handsome, intelligent boy, Charles William seems to have established good friendships with the East India captains who taught him his trade. After his father's death, he left the *Pacific* to sail to the West Indies on board the *Betsey* with Captain Prince. His third ship was the *Halswell,* another Indiaman. As he advanced in his training he was transferred to positions open on other vessels in the East India service, and there followed three voyages with Captain Cotton in the *Royal Charlotte* and a voyage with a Captain Larison. Next he sailed under Captain Wakefield in the *Lacelles.* When Charles was in London, he lived at the St. Paul's Coffee House, kept by a Mr. Shien whose son accompanied Charles when he left the India service. At age 26, Charles was presented with the

Captain Charles William Barkley.

opportunity to command his own vessel, the *Loudoun*, in the employ of the Bengal Fur Company.

The monopoly over maritime trade and the licensing of British ships exercised by both the East India Company and the South Sea Company essentially closed off trade to private British ships. The power of the East India Company, and to a lesser extent the South Sea Company, was far reaching. The East India Company controlled everything east of the Cape of Good Hope. The authority of the South Sea Company extended from Cape Horn north along the west coast of America to the Arctic and 782 nautical miles into the Pacific. Acting, at one time, like a proxy for the

British government they waged war, incited rebellions, dethroned princes. The East India Company was not like a regular corporation; it was a heavily armed and imperialistic force and not to be trifled with. Unless a master was a direct employee, it was necessary to obtain licences from both companies in order to take part in the fur trade. The licensing was costly and restrictions stifling, for even with a licence a ship could trade in furs to China but could not purchase goods in China for the return trip to England. To travel in ballast was not profitable and the cost of the trip could not be offset by the sale of furs alone. Understandably these monopolies were resented, even by some of the companies' employees. Several sought ways of bypassing these cartels and formed private syndicates under Portuguese or Austrian flags. The East India Company Court of Directors was well aware that British ships were sailing under foreign flags of convenience in order to evade the regulations and licensing. Trading without the necessary licensing would amount to poaching; if caught, ships could be confiscated and heavy fines levied on any who undertook such a venture. Captain John Meares, an English fur trader, sailed illegally under the Portuguese flag to the Northwest Coast in the *Nootka*, bypassing licensing by both the East India and South Sea companies. Meares, however, was astute in such matters, a manipulator and master of subterfuge, and called on a network of investors and other merchants of the East India Company, including Sir John Macpherson, governor-general of India, to sponsor a fur-trading expedition under the seeming protection of the East India Company. Despite this stranglehold on British merchant trade, private trade flourished and by the late 18th century there were nearly 13,000 English and Scottish private vessels.

Thus in India, in January of 1786, a group of British merchants, headed by J. H. Cox, a businessman based in Canton, formed the Bengal Fur Company, intending to exploit the fur resources discovered by Captain Cook on the northwest coast of North America. In March the new company dispatched two vessels from India, the *Nootka* commanded by Captain John Meares and the *Sea Otter* with William Tipping as master. The *Sea Otter* was lost with all hands and the *Nootka* became ice-bound in Prince William Sound where she lost all but nine of her crew from scurvy and alcohol poisoning due to Meares' lax control over the liquor stores. By May, with the warmer weather, two rival fur-trading ships were sailing in the area; the *Queen Charlotte* with Captain Dixon in command and the *King George* with Nathaniel Portlock, master and commander of the expedition. Dixon came to the assistance of Meares but he and Portlock surmised that Meares was trading illegally; they made him sign a bond of £500 and required him to cease trading. For many independent traders, however, the risk was outweighed by the price the pelts would fetch: Meares received $40 Spanish dollars per pelt for a total of $14,000. The price varied considerably depending upon the market conditions and Portlock and Dixon, trading just a few weeks, later managed only $19 per skin.

Two others had thought to exploit the fur trade by bypassing the system; John Reid, a naturalized Austrian subject appointed Austrian consul in Canton, and Daniel Beale, a naturalized Prussian and the Prussian consul in the same city. These are the men who persuaded Charles Barkley to resign from the East India Company and join them in a private fur-trading venture.

It is difficult to understand why Charles decided to leave the employ of the East India Company. Being an East India Company commander was a coveted position and had high social standing. This was the golden era of British maritime trading and there was no service equal to that of the East India Company. The masters sailed the finest ships in the trade, called Indiamen. They were superbly built, the pride of the British shipbuilding industry, in many ways better than the British navy ships, and were always well armed for protection against pirates and the warships of other nations. Their bluff bows and ample beam provided for a great deal of stability, and what they lacked in speed they made up for in appearance and comfort. The Indiamen were highly gilded and decorated with beautiful carving and were well furnished for the comfort of the crew.

Remaining in the employ of the East India Company would have guaranteed Charles a relatively affluent life. To be sure, a commission with the East India Company was expensive — some cost as much as £8,000 to £10,000 — but in exchange the masters received a monthly stipend as long as they were with the company, something the private trade could not match. They also received primage, a percentage of the total earnings made during the voyage, and while in port their pay was supplemented for expenses equivalent to five shillings a day, with an additional allowance for their table of five guineas, and a fine house if needed. Every detail was attended to. There were other benefits as well: the East India Company

An Indiaman in a shipyard on the Thames River.

was traditionally generous and contributed additional wine and food for the voyages, masters could make extra money on the side by taking passengers and charging whatever they wanted and they could supplement their income handsomely by private trade.

Perhaps it was the chance for Barkley to gain command of his own ship; maybe he wanted adventure or simply gave way to persuasive lobbying on the part of Messieurs John Reid and Daniel Beale. Barkley was to invest £3,000 of his own money in the outfitting of the *Loudoun*, under construction in a shipyard on the Thames River, the leading shipbuilding area in Britain. In order to evade the high fees due to the East India Company, the *Loudoun* was to be outfitted in a foreign port, given a new name, and fly Austrian colours under the new and questionable Austrian East India Company. Consequently, in August of 1786, Charles was in London overseeing the completion of the *Loudoun* in Shadwell Dock. He recorded progress in the back of a new logbook. On August 24 he wrote:

> Employed seeing all clear for getting the ship out of Dock at high water. Made an attempt but had not water enough. AM, rec'd on board 42 empty butts. People employed rafting them under the bottom.

The entry for the 25th reported:

> Got out of dock and worked her into Shadwell dock. 60 tons
> of ballast and two barrels of beer. People employed on sundry jobs
> about the rigging.

The last entry in the Shadwell Dock record was written on Friday, September 7, 1786, and on the following day they let slip the lines and rode the outgoing tide down the Thames, the wind filling the sails for the first time, as the *Loudoun,* 400 tons[12] and carrying 20 guns, sailed for Ostend. Within six weeks of his arrival in Ostend, Charles and Frances were married, and five weeks later the *Loudoun* had been renamed the *Imperial Eagle* and was ready for departure. Frances wrote:

> Charles William Barkley was brought up in the Honourable
> East India Company's sea service, but at the above period, he
> commanded the Ship *Loudoun,* fitted out and bound for the
> North West Coast of America on a Mercantile speculation. We
> accordingly sailed from the Harbour of Ostend on or about the
> bound Round Cape Horn.

Thus the adventure began: the log records that on Friday, November 24, 1786, at one o'clock in the afternoon, on a day with a fresh breeze and a bright haze, the crew of the newly renamed *Imperial Eagle* let go the ropes and made sail. The outgoing tide caught the ship and the distance between the figures on the dock and the young woman on the deck grew rapidly wider. Sailing ships are silent, so voices can be heard, shouting farewells. Frances Barkley began her new life aboard the ship, with Charles, and Henry Folger and William Miller, the first and second officers, and John Beale the purser, and Mr. Shien from St. Paul's Coffee House; the sailors would soon be as well known to her as members of her own family. The European coast shrank to a thin line along the horizon, then disappeared, and the wide sea stretched out, meeting the sky at the horizon all around them.

Chapter Two
The First Voyage: From Ostend to the Northwest Coast of North America

*W*hen Frances married Captain Charles Barkley and stepped aboard the *Imperial Eagle* she was at the vanguard of a small but growing number of wives who accompanied their husbands sailing in the merchant trade. Her life had changed abruptly. The sheltering convent walls had vanished and 17-year-old Frances Barkley found herself married to a man she hardly knew, aboard a small ship bound for unknown coasts, on a voyage which might last 10 years. Many young wives found that once they stepped on the deck of a ship their husbands became a stranger; a taskmaster, curt and sometimes brutal. It was a remarkable exploit for a young woman and there was no guarantee that Frances would enjoy or even be able to handle the rigors of a life at sea. Life aboard can't have been easy; during the first months she experienced fierce Atlantic seas sweeping over the ship, Charles' near-death from a fever, and the unwanted attentions of the first officer who would be with the ship until it reached Canton.

Loneliness was a constant companion for the wife of a sea captain and her life was isolating. Her husband's status would prevent her from mingling with the crew and, even though the *Imperial Eagle* was a grand ship and the largest in the merchant fur trade, much of Frances' time would have been spent confined to a small portion of the ship. A few details are preserved in her great-granddaughter's account (based on the Diary and letters) which states that the accommodation aboard the ship consisted of a tiny saloon, with a table screwed to the deck in the centre of the room, and four cabins opening off, two on each side; a cabin each for Charles, Frances and the chief mate, and the steward's pantry. The beds were narrow bunks and there was a small washing stand and a mirror against the bulkhead. Frances kept her clothes in a locker drawer under the bunk. The sailors acted as washerwomen and the rigging served as a clothesline; a cook prepared the meals.

The risks at sea were extreme. Charts were not available or were inaccurate, and navigational instruments were imperfect. The ships always leaked, for they were not securely caulked; thus, the statement that a ship "sprang a leak" would indicate that a veritable gaping hole had appeared. Crews lived on a deck built below the maindeck, in a small area at the bow of the ship, where their hammocks were slung close-packed, and where seas over the bow would come dripping through the deck above. The toilet for the crew consisted of a few slats hung over the sea at the bow, deluged by icy torrents when the weather was bad. The bilges of sailing ships always contained plenty of excrement because livestock — cows, pigs, goats, chickens — for food for the ship were kept on deck, since there was no better way of preserving them until they were to be eaten. Tubs of urine on deck were used for extinguishing fires, a very great threat on the wooden ships. The stench must have been fairly strong, for ships in an anchorage would manoeuvre to avoid being downwind of a particularly offensive vessel. It is therefore easy to understand why, in the log of the *Imperial Eagle,* the sailors are so frequently at work swabbing the decks. The filth and water leaking down through the vessel collected in the lowest part of the hold, called the well, and from there hand pumps removed it. The well could also collect gases (methane and sulphuretted hydrogen) and there was a standing warning about not going down into the well without first lowering a lighted lantern.

When the weather was bad, the crew would be damp and cold with no way to get dry, no heat anywhere. The cookroom or kitchen ("galley" is a term introduced at a later date) was always a serious fire hazard, for it was impossible to build a brick area in which the bricks were not in contact with the wooden timbers; in rough weather no fires were lit and there was no cooked food. Boiling was the routine method of cooking. Because of the overall dampness of the ships, it was difficult to keep bread or powder dry, and weevils flourished in the damp bread. C. S. Forester wrote that naval men always rapped the biscuit on the table to knock out the weevils, and if you tapped gently they came out of their own accord, fat white weevils with black heads.

Seafaring was a young man's occupation, for the hard work in bad conditions aged men rapidly. The *Bounty* list of mutineers in 1787 shows that the average age of the men was 26 years, and their average height only five feet six inches. Inguinal hernia was common, caused by such heavy tasks as heaving aboard the water casks, handling the weight of wet sails and turning the capstan to haul up the anchor. The worst health hazard was no longer scurvy and there is no evidence that any of Captain Barkley's men died of this dietary disease. James Lind, a naval surgeon, in 1754 published a treatise on scurvy in which he recommended the use of oranges, lemons, green vegetables and onions as certain cures. Unfortunately, the provision of these foods was sometimes impossible, and old eating customs tended to continue. "Son of a sea cook" is an extremely derogatory term for obvious reasons.

Frances could not have foreseen the hardships she would endure but she must have known something about the challenges that faced her; from a previous voyage she knew that she did not get seasick. But why would a young woman have been prepared to make such accommodations in her life? It is possible that she described her emotions in her Diary but if so, she did not transfer the words to her *Reminiscences*. Something about a seafaring life obviously appealed to Frances. Possibly she was intrigued by adventure and sailing to exotic ports. She had proved her adaptability somewhat for she had already lived in a number of cultures, and she might not have minded the isolation, having experienced some restrictions while at school in a convent. Then too, for Frances to stay at home would have meant not being with her husband for a number of years and, as correspondence was spotty, it might be years before she found out if she had been widowed. Also, as captain, Charles was expected to invest a substantial sum of his own money in the venture, which would mean he would not have sufficient funds to set Frances up in her own house; she would have had to live off the largesse of her family. For Frances and others like her, there was no option of staying ashore, no matter the challenges.

Her all-too-brief honeymoon was to end abruptly for on the third day out, fresh breezes and squally winds were recorded in the log and the topsails had to be close-reefed. The next day's weather was "fresh gales and flying clouds" and day by day the storm grew worse until it was recorded as "strong gales and heavy squalls" with rain, thunder and lightning. Finally it was necessary to heave to under reefed sails and mizzen staysails while the topgallant masts were struck, lest they be blown away. Chickens, ducks and turkeys were swept off the deck by the crashing seas.

Not once in her *Reminiscences* does Frances write a word of fear or apprehension as she faced the challenges of the voyages. She mentions the storm in her calm sentence:

> On the _____ we touched at the Cape de Verde Islands, where we got plenty of live stock and provisions, which were very acceptable as we had lost a vast number of Poultry in the Bay of Biscay, where we had experienced a violent Gale of Wind.

In contrast, the novelist Tobias Smollett wrote in 1748 of a similar departure from Europe:

> Set sale for the West Indies. Got away with a prosperous breeze … but this state of inaction did not last long … our main top-sail was split by a wind which in the morning increased to a hurricane. I was wakened by a most terrible din occasioned by the play of gun-carriages upon the deck above, the cracking of the cabins, the howling of the wind through the shrouds, the confused noise of the ship's crew, the pipes of the boatswain and his mate, the trumpets of the lieutenants, and the clanking of the chainpumps … I went above … the sea was swelled into billows mountain-high, on the top of which our ship sometimes hung as if it was about to be precipitated to the abyss below! Sometimes we sunk between two waves that rose on each side higher than our topmasthead and threatened by dashing together to overwhelm us in a moment! … a number of officers and sailors ran backward and forward with distraction in their looks, hallooing to one another, and undetermined what they should attend to first. Some clung to the yards, endeavouring to unbend the sails that were split into a thousand pieces flapping in the wind; others tried to furl those that were yet whole; while the masts, at every pitch, bent and quivered like twigs, as if they would have shivered into innumerable splinters …[1]

The scene aboard the *Imperial Eagle* was probably somewhat similar on the raging sea of December 10, 1786, when the ship hove to in order to take down the topgallant masts. If Frances was frightened, no word of it survives. In the space left after the mention of the violent Gale of Wind, she wrote, in a different ink:

(sadly at a loss for Dates to be filled up at some future period)

before she continued:

We had a long passage from thence, in consequence of bafling Winds on the Line, and my dear Husband having caught a Violent Cold was laid up with a Rhumatic Fever, and being in Unskillful hands, there was little hope of his recovery. My situation was very critical at that time from the unprincipled intentions of the Chief Mate supported by the second Mate, who being a Lieutenant in his Magesties service ought to have had more honor.

The log makes no note of a stop at the Cape Verde Islands off the west coast of Africa to replace the lost chickens. Nor is it possible to detect in the log any indication of the illness Frances described, and certainly there is nothing to illuminate the remark about the "unprincipled intentions" of Henry Folger.

On January 4, 1787, the log records that they "spoke an American ship from Baltimore for the Cape of Good Hope who had seen one of the Cape Verde Islands and informed us St Jago bore ESE distance of seven leagues, but on second inquiry acquainted us he had made thirty three Leagues West since he saw the land. Bore away for the Night SW in consequence of his information." The sighting of friendly ships was always an occasion. Weather permitting, and with the deft hand of the helmsman, the ships would pass each other closely and exchange basic information; names, weather conditions, when they last left port and where they were bound. If they could get close enough they would pass on letters and engage in actual conversation; if not they would relay their "report" with signal flags. This was referred to as "speaking a ship." Besides providing helpful information for navigation, weather and other hazards, speaking a ship acted as a way of communicating its whereabouts to the ship's owners. The captains of the respective ships would report their contact immediately upon reaching port.

The *Imperial Eagle* continued southwest toward the Portuguese colony of Brazil. By now it was necessary to replenish the ship's stores and Captain Barkley needed time to convalesce. Illness, accidents and death were a constant threat for mariners and in the absence of a ship's doctor, the master was in charge of the medical chest. One can only wonder at the distress that Frances must have felt when Charles took sick. She would have to rely on her family's medical traditions to care for him. She might have had access to recipes taken from other ships' journals and logbooks. Castor oil, enemas, laudanum, camphorated spirits, ginger and capsicum were common remedies used to treat sickness. The idea was to purge the illness from the body. A popular recipe for cholera was to mix 1 part laudanum, 1 part camphorated spirits, 2 parts capsicum, and 2 parts tincture of ginger given in a half-teaspoonful in a wineglass of water. In the main, Frances would be dealing with conditions for which there was no general understanding as to cause; it was thought that foul air and wet clothing were the basis for most illnesses. She mentions little of this time, other than to say her husband recovered.

Captain Barkley, as I shall in the course of these Notes style him however got better, and was able to resume his duties as Commander of his Ship, and directed her course for the Brazells, in order to recruit his health, take in water and refreshments. The Portuguese Authorities did not like the appearance of the Ship, she having so many Guns mounted, with such a numerous Ships company, Officers in Uniform, A Boats Crew dressed alike, and the manner of managing the Oars, gave the whole an appearance of a Kings Sloop of War, so that they set a watch over her. But when they were given to understand that she was bound to the Pacific Ocean, and as they concluded on a Voyage of Discovery, they were altogether polite and attentive, allowed us a House on shore at St. Salvadore, or Bay of All Saints, a caraige to take us out airing.

Coming into port sometimes required great ceremony and propriety. While in port, wives played a significant part in the social life expected of the ship's master. A captain's wife was a woman of consequence and was expected to entertain. She would dress up in her finest and go calling on people ashore or act as hostess for visitors aboard, overseeing sumptuous repasts. Often the biggest and best parties were held on board while a ship was at anchor. From her writings we learn that Frances did entertain other ships' company, dignitaries, chiefs, princes and missionaries at their various ports of call.

Writing about their stop in Brazil, she continues:

> We received invitations from Families residing in the country, thinking it good for the Captains health. But at first he was too weak to be able to pay visits, so that those invitations which it was deemed absolutely necessary that I should accept, I was Chaparooned by Mr. Miller, the second Mate, who, being a leutinant in the Kings service, cut a dash, with his sword at his side and his Naval Uniform. It was on one of those occasions, when my youth and inexperience led to a very ludicrous adventure — to be related —

At this point Frances left two inches of paper blank; unfortunately she did not fill in the space at a later time, and nothing is known of the "ludicrous adventure."

All Saints Bay, on the eastern coast of Brazil, is a natural harbour 40 kilometres long by 30 kilometres wide, surrounded by the Reconcavo, a fertile coastal lowland. A main channel about two miles wide is dredged for the Atlantic entrance. Salvador, the principal seaport and capital of Bahia state, is on the peninsula that protects the bay from the Atlantic. In the early 18th century many African slaves were shipped to Salvador, to work the Portuguese sugar plantations, and at the time of Frances and Charles Barkley's visit, there was a wealthy and well-established Portuguese upper class ruling the colony.

> Having very much recovered his health and Spirits which naturally were of the most exuberant kind, fond of Company & Show when on shore, but a great Martinet on board, he determined upon giving the Governer (or ViceRoy, I believed he was styled), together with his Lady Donna Maria and his little Daughter, with a numerous suite of Officers and attendants, a fete on

board. They came on board in a splendid Barge. The Ship was Dressed as it is called, with the colours of all Nations, the yards manned, a salute fired, and a handsome collation prepaired, and after they had examined everything on board, they departed in the same style & ceremonies.

We had been entertained by this Gentleman & Family several times on Shore at the Government House, and the Young Lady performed on a Musical Instrument, which I never saw or heard of before or after. It was play'd on by Keys like a Peanoforte, but instead of the hammers striking strings or wires, it was fitted with Musical Glasses, and it had a most beautiful Harmonious sound. It was called an Harmonicon.[2] The Ladies spoke French which was a great relief to me, who did not understand a word of Portuguese at that time.

With the harmonicon concert Frances' account of the first voyage ends abruptly.

In the log is the information that on February 7 at San Salvadore, with a moderate breeze and an outgoing tide, the ship was cleared for sea and made sail, heading south toward the dangerous passage around Cape Horn, the place most feared by seafaring men. There is no easy way from Europe into the Pacific, but of all the routes, the one south of Cape Horn is the most notorious, a byword for danger and misery, feared for its winds and for the gigantic waves that they push around and around the world without hindrance. Winds of over 72 kilometres per hour blow on 22 days out of 30, and ships from Europe had to tack into these bitter winds, able to make progress on a course of about seven compass points from the wind's direction. If the winds were very strong, the captain would have to wear ship, turning away from the wind and running before it while hauling the yards right around as far as they would go from one side to the other, with minimum sail set, then using great care to bring the ship up to the wind on the new tack. Running off like this lost miles, but to tack into the wind could be fatal, for a square-rigger's masts were set up and stayed to accept strong wind only from behind the vessel.

On March 3, 1787, the *Imperial Eagle* was within 15 miles of the latitude of the Falkland Islands. The entry of March 21 records "snow and sleet" and on the 22nd they saw "two penquins with several other sea fowl about the ship." Day after bitter day they headed west and then north, keeping well south of the Horn and a safe distance off the coast of Chile, a lee shore. Sailors feared the lee shores, where even a temporary loss of control would threaten shipwreck.

Once round the Horn the *Imperial Eagle* would have fallen off to the north until they could pick up the southeast trades which would take them to the doldrums near the equator. The doldrums sometimes saw ships becalmed for days if not weeks. Barkley would use this time to wash down the decks and holds with vinegar and air out the bedding, clothing and sails. During these long ocean passages when time would hang heavy for her, Frances might have occupied her time by sewing, reading or writing in her diary. A wife's basic job at sea was to keep her husband company. One of her granddaughters was to recall that Frances talked with great pleasure of the happy evenings when Charles would give up the command to Mr. Folger, the chief mate, and she would give Charles French lessons, by the soft light of tallow candles enclosed in thick glass.

To help pass the time some wives were taught navigational skills by their husbands and would assist with the ship's navigation and reckoning; some made and repaired sails while others helped to keep the logbook. Learning such skills would not have been unusual for Frances, for they were perfectly acceptable pastimes for captains' wives. From her detailed descriptions of weather conditions, it is more than likely that Frances not only learned to decipher weather patterns but also had a good command of meteorological principles.

Out of the doldrums the *Imperial Eagle* would pick up the northeast trades which took them to Hawaii. Sailing to the northwest coast via Hawaii was actually the quickest route; the square-riggers were downwind ships and it was impossible for them to sail against the northerly winds that prevail off the west coast of North America. Consequently Hawaii became a mid-ocean place for resupply. Here they could rest and restock their diminishing stores, taking on fresh water, yams, coconuts, salt, rope, hogs and plantains. The islands were also a good source for making up crew that had been lost to sickness; the local people or Kanakas made excellent seamen and many would join the ships trading to distant shores.

As the weather grew warmer their spirits rose. On May 19 the *Imperial Eagle* reached Hawaii. The log reads, "Shore about 5 or 6 Leagues. A.M. came off a great number of canoes and traded for hogs at the rate of a large nail per head." Exchanging a nail for a hog seemed an astounding bargain, then and now. Trading was active for several days. On May 24: "Came alongside several canoes with fishs. One of the natives remained on board, signifying an inclination to go in the ship." The Hawaiian native who remained on board was a girl named Winée, who became a servant to Frances and stayed with the ship until it reached Macao. When the supplies of food and water were replenished, the anchor was hauled up and the *Imperial Eagle* sailed for the northwest coast of North America.

On June 3, Captain Barkley's log reads "Light Breezes and pleasant weather. Punished John Willey with 1 Doz. lashes for Insolence." Barkley ran a tight ship and was well respected; this was the only example of such punishment recorded in the surviving sections of the Barkley logs. Crews were difficult to come by, many English seaman avoiding the long and perilous voyages as akin to a death sentence. Survival rates were low and there was little likelihood of seeing their home port again. Consequently most seamen were obtained by crimpers, the soul-sellers or human sharks who hung around the city docks, plucking unsuspecting rogues, drunks, derelicts and felons from their surroundings and selling them into the merchant trade. Because these seamen were considered a disagreeable and unruly lot, the use of harsh measures to maintain discipline was authorized and supported by both law and seafaring tradition. Punishments were graded according to the severity of the crime. Fisticuffs would merit time spent in irons with only bread and water, a knife fight would get a sailor a dunking three times from the yardarm for the first offence and keelhauled for the second offence. Killing another would find the guilty party tied to his victim and pitched overboard.

Winée.

In the fine weather of late May in 1787, the *Imperial Eagle* approached North America. The June 4 entry in the log noted "great quantities of small blubber commonly called Portuguese men of war." In the following days flocks of land birds were seen and "several grampus" (whales). The last entry is dated June 11 and is written on the first side of the page only. The other side is blank. It is not known what became of the rest of the log of the *Imperial Eagle,* and Captain Barkley's Journal has also disappeared. However, it is most fortunate that Frances Barkley's Diary was used by Captain John Walbran, for it is in the pages of Walbran's article "The Cruise of the *Imperial Eagle*" that some of the events of the next few months can be followed.

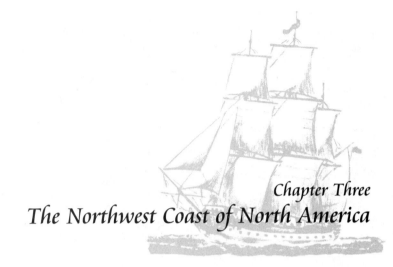

Chapter Three
The Northwest Coast of North America

*I*n June of 1787 the *Imperial Eagle* was the first European ship to sail into Nootka Sound that season. Surrounded by masses of islands, uncharted shoals, strong currents, extreme tides and fog-laced shores, the sound was tricky to navigate, particularly for a large Indiaman like the *Imperial Eagle*. At 400 tons she was the largest ship to enter these waters. Most ships that visited were the smaller 100- to 300-ton, two-masted, square-rigged vessels like snows or brigs. Her size may have kept Captain Barkley from exploring the small coves of the coast but not the inlet 71 nautical miles south of Nootka Sound, to which he gave his name, nor the larger, fabled Juan de Fuca Strait, entrance to the mainland coast.

Covering an area of approximately 800 square kilometres, Barkley Sound is the soul of the west coast of Vancouver Island, exposed as it is to the full sweep of the Pacific Ocean. Rough seas and heavy swells are the norm. To-day, some 200 years after the Barkleys' visit the sound is enjoyed by kayakers, boaters, campers and hikers, many of whom do not know of Captain Barkley and his discovery. Yet the reminders are there: Loudoun Channel, Imperial Eagle Channel, Trevor Channel and Cape Beale, named after the ship's purser, John Beale, who was killed on a trading expedition up the coast. All bear testimony to the silent footsteps of a man, a woman and a voyage long ago.

Thirty-nine nautical miles south of Barkley Sound is Juan de Fuca Strait. First discovered in 1592 by Juan de Fuca, the strait had proved elusive until Barkley rediscovered and charted its position. Questions abounded about

The Imperial Eagle *nears the west coast in a gale, with double-reeled topsails and single-reefed foresail. Painted by Steve Mayo.*

Juan de Fuca's earlier discovery. Was this the western entry to the Northwest Passage? Did such a strait even exist? Cook didn't think so — he dismissed it firmly — but Barkley's discovery put an end to such conjecture. It was a significant find, for it opened the way for others to explore and chart Vancouver Island and Puget Sound. Up to this point most mariners thought the coastline they had been visiting was part of the mainland, not an island.

Frances was now at the outer edges of the trading world, with little information available to guide her in her approach to the First Peoples of this coast. As the first European woman to reach these shores how would she be perceived? She may or may not have read Cook's writings about the people who populated this coast. If she did she did not give any indication. The one thing the Barkleys probably knew was that the pelts they sought could not be bought for a few glass beads; they would be dealing with shrewd traders. They wanted items that had meaning and use within their societies and were not quick to give away their furs. Metals such as iron, copper and brass were highly valued but even here quality was important. More than one trader was dismayed to see prime pelts escape for want of quality goods with which to purchase them.

Frances writes little in her *Reminiscences* about their first voyage to the Northwest Coast. Much of what is known is from the writing of Captain John Walbran who apparently had access to the original Diary. Captain Walbran, in command of the Canadian government steamship *Quadra*, spent 12 years, from 1892 to 1904, exploring the British Columbia coastline. He carried out many of the functions of today's Coast Guard, making hydrographic charts, and was fascinated by the history of the region.

The *Victoria Colonist*, on March 3, 1901, published Captain Walbran's account of the trading voyage of the *Imperial Eagle*, "taken chiefly from the original diary kept by his young wife, Frances Hornby Barkley (née Trevor), the first white woman to visit the shores of what is now Vancouver Island. The diary is in the possession of her grandson Captain Edward Barkley R.N. (retired) residing at Westholme, Vancouver Island, B.C." Walbran related the facts about the voyage from Ostend to the Sandwich Islands (Hawaii):

> ... and from thence the ship steered for Nootka Sound ... where the
> ship arrived in the month of June 1787, the day previously to
> making the land a dreadful storm from the south-east having been
> encountered. No other vessels were in the sound, and apparently

Habitations at Nootka Sound. Drawn by John Webber, 1778.

none in the immediate vicinity, consequently Capt. Barkley did extremely well with his trade and soon procured, mainly though the following circumstance, all the furs the Indians had for sale.

The Barkleys were at the earlier end of the fur trade and consequently did well. But as trading increased so did the price of the furs, particularly at the places most commonly visited by the merchant traders. As a result the furs traded at Nootka were found to cost more than at other places. In 1786 Meares traded one piece of copper for ten skins; the rate by 1792 was one piece of copper for one skin. Also the pelts quickly saturated the Canton market and prices fell accordingly.

Walbran's article continues:

Shortly after the ship had moored in Friendly Cove a Canoe was paddled alongside and a man in every respect like an Indian and a very dirty one at that, clothed in a greasy sea-otter skin, came on board, and to the utter astonishment of Capt. and Mrs. Barkley introduced himself as Dr. John Mackey late surgeon of the trading brig, *Captain Cook*. This visitor informed them that he had been living at Nootka amongst the Indians for the previous twelve months, during which time he had completely conformed himself to their habits and customs, which Mrs. Barkley in her diary emphatically states were disgusting. Dr. Mackey had learned the language and also had made himself acquainted more or less, with the surrounding country, thus making his services of great value to Capt. Barkley, who, before the ship left the sound, engaged Dr. Mackey as trader, a duty which he seems to have carried out to Capt. Barkley's entire satisfaction, that gentleman frequently boasting to Mr. Etches, the supercargo of the *Prince of Wales* and *Princess Royal,* who arrived later, what an excellent cargo they had secured on the *Imperial Eagle* through Mackey's influence with the Indians.

The *Imperial Eagle* had been but a short time in the sound, when two vessels arrived from England, the ship *Prince of Wales* and sloop *Princess Royal,* commanded respectively by Capts. Colnett and Duncan. These vessels were ten months out from England, having left London long before the *Imperial Eagle* left Ostend, and their crews were extremely sick with scurvy. The *Princess Royal* was only 50 tons burden and manned by fifteen men, yet she had made the long voyage round Cape Horn with the larger ship. Arriving in such a snug harbor, Friendly Cove, and finding there a well found and disciplined ship like the *Imperial Eagle* was a great boon to both these vessels as £100 worth of wine, tobacco, portable soup and other luxuries was at once kindly allowed them by Capt. Barkley from his well plenished stores.

Captain George Dixon, in his book *A Voyage Round the World, but More Particularly to the North-West Coast of America … in the* King George *and* Queen Charlotte, dated 1789, has written another account of the meeting at Nootka Sound, or King George's Sound as it was then named. Captains Dixon and Portlock, sent out by the King George's Sound Company, held the necessary licences from the East India Company. This association of merchants also dispatched the ships *Prince of Wales* and *Princess Royal,* mentioned in the following excerpt:

Mr. John Etches, brother to our managing owner, (who was on board the *Prince of Wales)* informed me that they had been near a month in King George's Sound, but had done very little business, having found a ship there called the *Imperial Eagle,* commanded by a Captain Berkley. She sailed from Ostend the latter end of November 1786, and arrived at King George's Sound near a month before the *Prince of Wales* and *Princess Royal.* Captain Berkley frequently boasted to Mr. Etches what an excellent cargo of skins he had purchased, and indeed there is some reason to suppose that he had been tolerably successful from the following circumstances.

Two vessels from Bombay were at King George's Sound in the summer of 1786, and left one of their people behind; this man was found here by Captain Berkley, who gave the following account of him:

His name is John M'Key; he was born in Ireland, and went to Bombay in the East India Company's service. Two vessels (viz. the *Captain Cook*, Captain Lorie; and the *Experiment,* Captain Guise) were fitting out in 1785, on an expedition to the North West coast of America; that he engaged on board the *Captain Cook* as Surgeon. They sailed from Bombay the 28th of November, 1785, and arrived at King George's Sound the 27th of June, 1786. That being very ill of a purple fever he was left behind for the recovery of his health, at the request of Mr. Strange, the Supercargo to both vessels. Mr. Strange desired him to learn the language and to ingratiate himself with the natives, so that if any other vessels should touch there he might prevent them from purchasing any furs, promising at the same time to return for him the ensuing spring. That the two vessels procured 600 prime sea otter skins during their stay here, and left the Sound the 27th of July, intending to sail for Cook's River. That the *Sea Otter,* Captain Hanna, from China, arrived at King George's Sound in August, 1786, and that Captain Hanna offered to take him on board, which he refused, alledging, that he began to relish dried fish and whale oil, was satisfied with his way of life, and perfectly contented to stay 'till next year, when he had no doubt of Mr. Strange sending for him: that Captain Hanna left the Sound in September. That the natives had stripped him of his cloaths, and obliged him to adopt their mode of dress and filthiness of manners; and that he was now a perfect master of their language, and well acquainted with their temper and disposition. He had made frequent incursions into the interior parts of the country about King George's Sound, and did not think any part of it was the Continent of America, but a chain of detached islands.

Mr. Etches (from whom I had this intelligence) assured me that no great dependance could be placed on M'Key's story, he being a very ignorant young fellow, and frequently contradicting himself; but that entire credit might be given to that part of it respecting his adopting the manners of the natives, as he was equally slovenly and dirty with the filthiest of them all. His knowledge of the language was greatly short of what be boasted; neither was he very contented in his situation, for he gladly embraced Captain Berkley's offer of taking him on board, and seemed delighted to think he was going to leave so uncomfortable a place: however, admitting him to be possessed of but an ordinary capacity, he certainly must be better acquainted with the people here, from more than a year's residence amongst them, than any occasional visitor could possibly be; and there can be no doubt but that Captain Berkley found him extremely useful in managing his traffic with the natives.[1]

Walbran comments:

In reference to this latter statement in which Mr. Etches the super-cargo referred to, gives his opinion of Mr. Mackey, the statement should not be greatly depended upon as impartial. It must be remembered that Mr. Etches who was a brother to the managing owner of the *Prince of Wales* and *Princess Royal*, and therefore doubtless greatly interested in the success of the voyage, had not been able to obtain many furs, if any, in Friendly Cove, and this fact alone would probably not allow him to view Mackey's conduct in a friendly light, especially if he attributed their ill-success to Mackey's exertions on behalf of the *Imperial Eagle*.

It should be noted that John Mackay was well treated by Maquinna, Chief Tsaxawasip of the Mowachaht tribe of the Nootka. Mackay was protected by Maquinna until he broke a taboo and stepped over the cradle of Maquinna's child. He was subsequently beaten and banished for a number of weeks. When the child died Mackay was exiled and left to survive on his own. When he was found by Barkley he was saved from Captains Portlock and Dixon who knew about Mackay and intended to charge him with poaching and take him in irons to Canton.

Although he was dismayed to find the *Imperial Eagle* at Friendly Cove and aware that the Barkley vessel was trading without East India Company authority, Captain James Colnett of the *Prince of Wales* was grateful for Captain Barkley's generosity with supplies. He wrote:

> The commander of the *Lowden* sent his boat twice with some deer, & he being in want of a little paint oil & some black varnish I spared it, & got some dead Eyes from them which we were Short of, the Ship's crew visited and were on a very friendly footing. Captain Barkley came on board me the thirteenth. I did not mention to him then the Illegality of his trading in the Southsea Company's limits, thinking it would have been a breach of Friendship, nor did I at that time think our situation so bad as it afterwards prov'd, for having no Copper which was the only exchange the Natives took for their Skins, he engrossed the whole trade & ruined ours. He was not Ignorant he had no right here as he fitted out in the [Thames] River at the time we did & went to Ostend for a Clearance.
>
> On the Eighteenth I sent a letter to Captain Berkley, by my chief mate, requesting he would shew him his Authority for trading in the Southsea Company's limits; my right for so doing carried with him, it was refus'd but several letters & Messages pass'd, but it being in a language my chief mate could not understand we remain'd as much uninform'd as ever, but himself & Crew being mostly Englishmen which is contrary to act of Parliament, it remains to be settled on our return to England. The man named Mackey that had been living on shore some months came one day on board with one of the *Lowden's* Mates but by some mistake I did not see him.
>
> I had now some thoughts of staying in the coast another season, & if so, some few of the articles Captain Berkley had offer'd me would be very acceptable to the Ship's Company & he repeating his services everytime the Boat went, I got him to spare me some little

matters with a hhd. [hogshead] & Quarter Cask of wine, & twenty Gallons of Brandy to be divided between us & the Sloop [the *Princess Royal*] sending the Supercargo' Bill on his Brother, the Owner, for payment. He very politely return'd me ye Bill desiring I would leave it till we met at China, taking the mates receipt for the things. Captain Berkley's behaviour was as humane & Generous as I ever met with, and I am sorry his Busyness so clash'd with mine that I was oblig'd to behave in the distant manner I did.

On the 24th [July] the *Lowden* sail'd.[2]

Captain Walbran's account continues:

Mrs. Barkley notes that in King George's Sound, as she always called Nootka, the climate was about the same as in Scotland, with perhaps a little more rain, and that the fruit they got ripened at a much more advanced season than the same berries did in England, or even in Scotland. She speaks well of the two chiefs, Maquilla and his brother Callecum; these men seemed to her more intelligent than the other Indians and also more active and enterprising. Readers of Meares' Voyage will recollect this chief Callecum was barbarously shot by the Spaniards in Friendly Cove about two years after the visit of the *Imperial Eagle*.

After a stay of a month in Friendly Cove[3] the cruise along the unknown coast to the south eastward was commenced, Mrs. Barkley noting in her diary that her husband was the first person to examine closely this shore line.

The diary states as follows: "A day or two after sailing from King George's Sound we visited a large sound in latitude 49.20 North, which Captain Barkley named Wickaninnish's sound, the name given it being that of a chief who seemed to be quite as powerful a potentate as Maquilla at King George's Sound. [This sound is now known as Clayoquot Sound.] Wickaninnish has great authority and this part of the coast proved a rich harvest of furs for us. Likewise, close to the southward of this sound, we came to another very large sound, to which Captain Barkley gave his own name, calling it Barkley Sound. Several coves and bays and also

Nootka people. Drawn by John Webber, 1778.

islands in this sound we named. There was Frances Island, after myself; Hornby peak, also after myself; Cape Beale after our purser; Williams point and a variety of other names, all of which were familiar to us. We anchored in a snug harbour in the island, of which my husband made a plan as far as his knowledge of it would permit. The anchorage was near a large village, and therefore we named the island Village Island. From here my husband sent the boats out to trade under the charge of Mr. Miller, second mate, and Mr. Mackey, and they were again very successful."

Captain Meares, using Captain Barkley's charts and following the track of the *Imperial Eagle* one year later, also described this anchorage, neglecting to mention that Barkley had discovered it. Only the sentence, "The long-boat was sent to find *the* anchoring ground," (italics added) suggests that Captain Meares had foreknowledge of its existence. Meares wrote:

> On the 11th, in the morning, we were off the mouth of this sound, which appeared extensive, but of no great depth. Several islands were placed nearly in the middle of it, which were rather high, and well wooded. The long-boat was sent to find the anchoring ground, and, above eleven o'clock, she returned to pilot us into a fine spacious port, formed by a number of islands, where we anchored in eight fathoms water, over a muddy bottom, and securely sheltered from wind and sea. A large number of natives immediately came off in their canoes, and brought abundance of fish, among which were salmon, trout, cray and other shell-fish, with plenty of wild berries and onions. These people belonged to a very large village, situated on the summit of a very high hill. This port we named Port Effingham in honour of the noble Lord of that title.[4]

Continuing Walbran's account:

> From Barkley Sound the *Imperial Eagle* again proceeded to the Eastward, and to the great astonishment of Capt. Barkley and his officers, a large opening presented itself, extending miles to the eastward with no land in sight in that direction.
>
> The entrance appeared to be about four leagues in width, and remained about that width as far as the eye could see. Capt. Barkley at once recognized it as the long lost strait of Juan de Fuca, which Captain Cook had so emphatically stated did not exist.

In his book *British Columbia Coast Names* Walbran wrote: "Juan de Fuca, whose real name was Apostolos Valerianos, a native of Cephalonia [the largest of the Ionian Islands, Greece] who seems to have been in his own day as neglected and misunderstood as he was afterwards doubted and ignored, and whose pretensions in regard to the exploration of these waters were so long scoffed at by geographers, was undoubtedly the discoverer of the strait which bears his name. *Purchas, his Pilgrimes* published 1625, states, in substance, as follows: 'In the year 1592 the Viceroy of Mexico sent a pilot named Juan de Fuca on a voyage of discovery to the northwest. De Fuca followed the coast until he came to the latitude of 47 degrees and there finding that a broad inlet trended to the eastward between the latitudes of 47° and 48°, he sailed up it for more than twenty days.' De Fuca found many islands in this inland navigation, and also a broad sea, much broader than at the entrance. He also noted 'to mark the entrance of the great inlet that on the northwest coast is a headland or island with an exceedingly high pinnacle or spired rock, like a pillar, thereupon.' This is substantially correct; the island is Tatooche, and the spired rock, now known as De Fuca's pillar, 150 feet high, stands in solitary grandeur, a little off shore, about two miles southwards of Tatooche Island."[5]

Captain Cook, in *A Voyage to the Pacific Ocean*, 1784, recorded his experience: "It is in this very latitude where we now were, that geographers have placed the pretended Strait of Juan de Fuca. We saw nothing like it; nor is there the least probability that ever such thing existed." Then Cook stood off the coast because of gale-force winds "so that instead of running in for

Caption James Cook. The original painting,, by Nathaniel Dance, is in the National Maritime Museum, Greenwich.

the land, I was glad to get an offing, or to keep that which we had already got."[6] Walbran observed:

It must be conceded however to that great seaman, that he had been blown off the coast in this very particular spot by a most violent hurricane and therefore must have just missed making the great rediscovery himself. The *Imperial Eagle* did not go up the strait, but kept along the ocean coast, which was now found to be compact and unbroken by bays or inlets. In latitude 47.43 a small island, a short distance from the mainland was met with, and between this island and the main shore the vessel anchored, the coast appearing to be inhabited. The long boat was hoisted out and sent in with another and smaller boat in tow to go up a small river which could be seen from the ship, in order to trade with the natives. The small boat was taken with the long boat in order to go up the stream should the water be too shoal for the larger boat. The long boat was in charge of Mr. Miller, the second mate, accompanied by Mr. Beale the purser, and ten men. The river was found too shallow, as expected, for the long boat, and the smaller boat with Mr. Miller, Mr. Beale and four seamen rowed away up the stream, taking with them a sheet of copper for purposes of trade. These unfortunate persons were never seen again, though every exertion was made by the long boat's crew to find them before returning to the ship.

The next day a strongly armed party was sent in search of the unfortunate people. A landing was effected and a careful search made, when to the horror of the searchers, some portions of the clothes and linen, mangled and bloody, were found, but no part of their bodies or boat, so the dreadful conviction was forced upon the *Imperial Eagle*'s company, that all had been murdered and their bodies eaten or burnt. This sad catastrophe much depressed everybody, and after naming the island Destruction Island (a name it still bears) and the river Destruction River [probably the Hoh River], Capt. Barkley determined to proceed to China with his good collection of furs amounting to eight hundred, the vessel arriving at Macao in December 1787.

The following year, Captain Meares recorded a sequel to the deaths of the six men of the *Imperial Eagle*'s company. He wrote that on June 8, 1788:

a strange canoe with several natives in it, came to Friendly Cove, where the *Iphigenia* was anchored. They offered for sale a human hand, dried and shrivelled up, the fingers of which were complete, and the nails long, but our horror may be better conceived than expressed when we saw a seal hanging from the ear of one of the men in the canoe which was known to have belonged to the unfortunate Mr. Miller of the *Imperial Eagle*. The seamen wished at once to wreak their vengeance on the murderers, as they believed them to be of Mr. Miller and his companions, and would certainly have carried out their threat, had it not been pointed out that the possession of the hand and seal might have been procured by the natives by the way of barter. This surmise proved to be correct, as next day Maquilla himself assured us on his own knowledge that the men in the canoe had received the articles, which had occasioned so much disgust and horror to us, in the way of trade from the natives of Queenhythe, the very place where Mr. Miller and his associates had been murdered nearly a year previously.[7]

Captain Barkley's men were neither the first nor the last to be attacked by the people living near the mouth of the Strait of Juan de Fuca. A boat's crew of the *Santiago* (Captain Bruno Hecata) had been killed at the mouth of the Moclips River in 1775, and Captain Meares, commanding the *Felice* in 1778, although warned by Chief Wickaninnish and having seen the withered hand offered for sale, sent out Robert Duffin to explore, in a small boat. Duffin was attacked but he and his men fought for their lives in a bloody hand-to-hand combat and managed to escape, although every man was wounded, some seriously.

As a former East India Company man, Barkley would have been trained, as Cook had been, to show respect to those they traded with, not because of any pretensions of equality or governing ideologies about the "noble savage," but because diplomacy made good business sense. In fact both Cook and later Vancouver had specific Admiralty instructions to be above reproach in

their interactions with local populations. Why then the seemingly unpro-
voked attack? Competition for the black, lustrous sea-otter pelts was fierce
and most traders made no more than a few voyages. Consequently, they had
little compunction to conduct themselves with due diligence. Some of the
independent fur traders would force trading and treat their hosts with hos-
tility and disdain. In many instances they disregarded local customs and pro-
tocol, ignored the chiefs and abused the women. It is not surprising that
reprisals took place, even on the innocent.

Frances did not record her undoubted shock and dismay; nor have the
pages of the log survived to detail the sad event which terminated the visit of
the *Imperial Eagle* to the northwest coast.

Chapter Four
China

*I*n July of 1787, the *Imperial Eagle* set sail for Canton, the company depressed and shocked by the loss of Mr. Beale, Mr. Miller and the four seamen, pawns in the game played for the skins of the ill-fated sea otter. For it was the innocent otter which lured those men to their deaths, half a world away from their homes.

During the 17th century, the tiny vessels of European explorers and traders had ventured into many remote and unknown parts of the globe, but only Juan de Fuca reached the British Columbia coast, and no European sails appeared along the North Pacific coast, with its thick fogs, terrible storms and endless rain. For thousands of years the First Nations people had lived undisturbed, weaving their rich, intricate cultural patterns, in harmony with the animals and plants that shared their raincoast kingdom. Among those animals was the otter, destined to be the first cause of the destruction of their world. It almost seems that there was an awareness of this, for the much-respected otter was the subject of a Tsimshian song which chanted:

> The otter is a source of pride and unquenched desire. It ends
> in ruin and perdition.

The sea otter is usually a little over one and a half (1.7) metres long and one metre in circumference at the breast bone. Describing the animal, Marius Barbeau, one of Canada's most renowned pioneering ethnographers

Sea otter. Drawn by Pat Wright.

and folklorists, wrote, "Seen when it is running, the gloss of its hair surpasses the blackest velvet."[1] George Steller, one of the first naturalists to describe the otter, spoke of its intelligence and tenderness: "the male caresses the female by stroking her, using the fore feet as hands … Their love for their young is so intense that they expose themselves to the most manifest danger of death. When their young are taken away from them, they cry bitterly like a small child and grieve. After ten to fourteen days they grow as lean as a skeleton, become sick and feeble, and will not leave the shore."[2] He described the otter playing with their young ones, throwing them and catching them again with joy. Meares wrote of seeing the otter, sometimes many leagues from land, sleeping on their backs on the surface of the water, with their young reclining on their breasts: "As the cubs are incapable of swimming till they are several months old, the mother must have some curious method of carrying them out to sea and returning them to their hiding places on shore, or in the cavities of rocks that project into the sea; indeed they are known to sleep with their young on their breast and to swim with them on their back; but if they should be unfortunately overtaken by the hunters, the dam and her brood always die together. She will not leave her young ones in the moment of danger and therefore shares their fate."[3] He also spoke of "the wonderful swiftness with which they swim" and commented on the jetty blackness and exceeding beauty of their fur. This lovely creature was all but totally exterminated, in only a few years, by European greed, to provide rich garments for czardom and royalty and to satisfy the pride of mandarins in China.

The Russians were the first to slaughter the otter, along the Siberian coast; and when they had decimated the otter population of the Kamchatkan peninsula they ventured farther, stone by stepping stone across the Kurile, Pribilov and Aleutian islands. Although some of these furs were sold in Europe, by far the highest profits were made by selling them to the Chinese. However, the rulers of the Celestial Kingdom viewed trade as inherently undesirable, allowing wealth to leave the country and exposing the Chinese people to dangerous contacts with degenerate barbarians. They sought to minimize the disadvantages by restricting trade to two points of entry: Kyakhta for Russian trade and Canton for trade with other nations.

When rumours of Russian expansion along the North Pacific rim reached the Spaniards, they dispatched from Mexico expeditions under Perez in 1774 and Bodega y Quadra in 1775. News of the Spanish voyages was carried to London by the English ambassador in Madrid, which inspired the English to send Captain Cook, on his third expedition, to re-establish the claims of Sir Francis Drake near San Francisco in 1579. It was the company of Cook's third expedition who discovered the secret wealth, almost by accident.

When Cook arrived at Nootka in 1778, the Indians offered the black, silky pelts of the otter in exchange for the fancy clothes, tools and weapons of the English sailors. Many months later, after Cook had been killed in Hawaii, when Cook's ships sailed into Canton his men were astounded to discover the high prices the Chinese would pay for these same skins. Captain King wrote:

> One of our seamen sold his stock, alone, for 800 dollars ... When it is remembered that the furs were, at first, collected without our having any idea of their real value; that the greatest part had been worn by the Indians, from whom we purchased them; that they were afterward preserved with little care and frequently used for bed clothes and other purposes during our cruise to the North; and that, probably, we had never got the full value of them in China; the advantages that might be derived from a voyage to that part of the American coast, undertaken with

commercial views, appears to me of a degree of importance sufficient to call for the attention of the public. The rage with which
our seamen were possessed to return to Cook's River and buy
another cargo of skins, to make their fortunes, at one time was not
far short of mutiny.[4]

It was like a coin dropped on the pavement of the world. All eyes swiv-
elled to the North Pacific and many men considered how they could get a
share of the vast wealth to be won by selling otter pelts to the Chinese.

Although they wanted the incomparable otter fur, the Chinese were by
no means as eager for trade as were the Europeans who arrived at the port of
Canton. The first to reach China, the Portuguese, in 1537 obtained Chinese
permission to occupy Macao, a tiny peninsula at the mouth of the Pearl
River, downstream from Canton. For upwards of half a century the Portuguese had exclusive trading rights, until the arrival of the Dutch, who were
allowed to build a factory (a trading post) just outside Canton. In the 17th
century an English factory was built next to the Dutch, and later other nations arrived. The land given for foreign factories was a putrid marsh, where
piles driven to great depths supported the "Thirteen Hongs," the factories of
Dutch, English, and later, Austrian, Swedish, Parsee, Danish, French and
other trading nations.

The Chinese were wisely suspicious
about allowing aggressive foreigners into
their country. However, they wanted
raw cotton from India, and otter pelts
from the North Pacific, and ginseng,[5]
and the foreigners were very eager to get
China's raw and manufactured silks, cotton cloth, porcelain, furniture (cabinets
and cases, lacquered and varnished),
boxes inlaid with mother-of-pearl, fans,
toys, tiger and panther skins, rubies,
white lead, vermilion, canes, tobacco,
rice, musk and, above all else, *tea*. A
craze for all things Chinese had swept
the European upper classes, and tea was

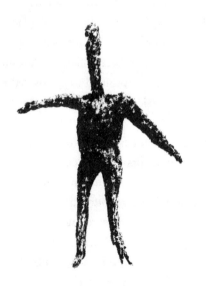

Ginseng root. Drawn by J. F. Whittingham.

The Approach to Canton.

establishing itself as the symbol of British social life. So the two doors to China, at Canton and Kyakhta, were kept open, under the close control of the Chinese government. Conducting an exchange in Canton was a complex procedure, however, as the Barkleys were to discover.

Captain Walbran states that the *Imperial Eagle* left the scene of the murders at the mouth of the Strait of Juan de Fuca on July 24 and reached Macao in December of 1787, but Captain Dixon wrote that the *Imperial Eagle* was in Macao when his ship *Queen Charlotte* arrived there in November. Constance Parker thought that they went to Alaska and then sailed to the Sandwich Islands (Hawaii) but were blown south where they landed on an island (part of an archipelago) and claimed it for England, calling it Barkley,

Great Temple, Macao.

which the natives pronounced Baroia. From there they proceeded to Macao, where a Mr. W. Cummins lent them a house. It is difficult to know how to evaluate the Constance Parker account of this part of the voyage.

Vessels approaching the Chinese coast first saw the massive shapes of junks, their sails like enormous bats — both heavy sea-going junks and the livelier and more manoeuvrable light fishing junks. At the entrance to the Pearl River, pilots came on board to guide the vessel through the gap in the bar. Vessels then anchored off Macao, and the longboats splashed into the river to take the captains ashore to deal with port officials. Nothing is known about the Mr. Cummins who loaned the Barkleys a house, but it was certainly necessary to make arrangements for Frances to stay at Macao, as no foreign women were permitted to proceed beyond that point. This would not have been thought unusual by Frances as it was common practice for the wives to board out, usually with an expatriate or family of the same nationality. After the arrangements were made Charles took the ship to the anchorage at Whampoa, and then arranged the transport of himself and the furs to Canton, to the factories just outside the city.

As Frances waited for her husband to conduct business she could take advantage of the rare opportunity to attend to the personal necessities that life at sea made difficult, if not impossible. She could properly dress her hair, attire herself in more fashionable clothing, shop for stylish materials, and have time for more genteel pleasures; entertainment and afternoon repasts would certainly have been on the agenda. With any luck, letters and news from home would be waiting for her and she would have the leisure to catch up on her correspondence. The sense of detachment that came from spending many months at sea could, for the moment at least, fade into distant memory.

Illustrations from a book published in 1843, entitled *China, in a series of views* (drawn from original authentic sketches by Thomas Allom Esq.) give some idea of the important cities of Macao and Canton at that period. Although the precise date of Allom's sketches is not known, the main buildings in the scenes were probably constructed before 1787, and the land forms were certainly unchanged. The city of Macao occupied a position of beauty rather than strength. It stood upon a peninsula three miles long by one mile wide, one side of which curved into a beautiful bay. The ridge of this rocky point and its sloping sides were covered with churches, convents, turrets and tall houses. A narrow sandy isthmus joined the peninsula to the heights of Heang-shan, which were defended with forts manned by the Chinese. A wall crossed the isthmus to separate the foreigners from the Chinese. A presiding Chinese mandarin lived in Macao to make sure that the Portuguese forts were not strengthened, nor the garrison of about 400 men enlarged. The Portuguese authorities at Macao consisted of a military governor, a judge and a bishop,

The Pria Granda, Macao.

but the Chinese portion of the population (about 30,000 Chinese in 1840 in comparison with 4,000 foreigners) was subject to Chinese authority only.

The Pria Granda was a promenade following the sweep of the shore, backed by a row of handsome houses. There stood the residence of the Portuguese governor, the Customs House, the Senate House, English houses, Portuguese churches and Chinese temples. The scene shows no large vessels, for the inner harbour was shallow and exposed to storms, the roadstead for safe anchorage being at Whampoa, 16 kilometres closer to Canton.

Whampoa, one of a group of islands, was the European anchorage near the mouth of the Pearl River. Allom's drawing shows the anchorage as seen from Dane's Island, looking westward toward Canton, with many foreign vessels riding at anchor. The crews were permitted to land and enjoy the islands, and there was one island ceded to foreigners as a burial ground (upon payment, however, of high fees). Canton Reach extends in a westerly direction, enclosed on the north by a range of hills.

Trade was conducted in a formal manner. Upon arrival of a vessel at Whampoa, the Chief Customs officer went on board to receive an elaborate meal and expensive gifts. This dignitary established the nature of the vessel's cargo, pocketed a considerable fee (ostensibly on the emperor's behalf) and departed, whereupon a Chinese boat arrived to take the captain, several members of the crew and the cargo of furs to Canton. This was a pleasant journey, made to the sing-song chants of the Chinese boatmen as they pushed their

Whampoa, showing foreign ships at anchor, as seen from Dane's Island.

European factories on the Pearl River at Canton.

craft upriver with long poles, along the narrowing river, with green hills rising on either side. Finally, through a swarm of sampans, the flags of the European trading posts could be seen, fluttering against the sky. At the factories there were goods from every country in the world — sacks full of gold and silver coin from America or Spain, bales of fragrant spices, cases of opium, snow-white Indian cotton, and the strange objects from Britain, which were treated as amusing toys.

China had a contempt for all things Western, and trade was rigidly institutionalized with a view to minimizing contact with foreigners. Trade was controlled by the emperor through a Chinese merchants' guild, the Co-hung, a group of 10 to 13 merchants given a charter in 1760. Like every foreign ship, the *Imperial Eagle* was required to have a sponsoring merchant or *fiador*, who became the surety for the good behaviour of the ship's company. This compelled Charles to confine his business to one house, or *hong*. By the time he paid the high port duties and other fees (the measurage fee, the "cumshaw" or present, the pilotage fee, the linguist's fee, the *comprador*'s fee for services in the provisioning of the vessel, rent for storage space in the factory, stevedore charges, import and export duties, weighing fees and a surtax), it was obvious that the Chinese, though considering trade undesirable, had nevertheless arranged matters to provide maximum profits with a minimum of interference from the barbarians at their door.

A house near Canton.

The ancient city of Canton was enclosed by a wall only six miles long, but the population of the city and suburbs, together with the people living on junks on the Pearl River, was estimated to have been about one million in 1840. A street scene in Canton shows how the streets resembled flagged courts and passages, with large granite flagstone paving. There were no wheeled carriages. The streets sometimes contracted to the breadth of a doorway and at certain places iron gates were hung to lock up separate streets at night. Houses were seldom higher than two storeys, and were built of brick, wood or, for the poorest class, clay. Wares were displayed for sale with confidence in public honesty, shaded from the sun by umbrellas and bamboo shades. At nightfall the charming lanterns suspended over every door cast a soft light.

The success of Charles' negotiations with the Cantonese merchants was recorded in Captain George Dixon's *A Voyage Round the World* published in London in 1789. Captain Dixon found the *Imperial Eagle* in the Pearl River when he arrived there in November of 1787. He wrote:

> At ten o'clock in the evening a Chinese boat came alongside, bringing a Mr. Folger on board; he was the Chief Mate of the vessel we had seen in the Roads, and which proved to be the *Imperial Eagle,* Captain Berkley, who, thou mayest remember,

was seen by Captain Colinett in King George's Sound. In consequence of a quarrel with Captain Berkley, he had left him and been at Macao, where, meeting with Captain Dixon, he had procured a passage with us to Canton.

We learned from Mr. Folger that the *Imperial Eagle* left Ostend on the 23rd of November, 1786, and that King George's Sound was the farthest they had been to Northward on the coast. They procured a good many valuable skins a degree or so to the Southward of King George's Sound; and their cargo consisted of nearly seven hundred prime skins, and many of inferior value. In the course of their trade they met with a most melancholy accident.[6]

Dixon repeated the account of the disappearance of Beale, Miller and the four seamen. Henry Folger, first officer of the *Imperial Eagle* was the same person of whom Frances commented, during Charles' illness on the Atlantic, "My situation was very critical at that time from the unprincipled intentions of the Chief Mate," and it would therefore seem probable that both Charles and Frances were satisfied to see the departure of Mr. Folger at Macao.

It may have been at this time that the Barkleys acquired a bamboo chair of a type made in Canton from 1760 on for sale to Europeans. This unusual chair

A street in Canton.

The Barkley chair, made in Canton about 1760.

has survived the Barkleys' travels by sea and their many moves in England as well as the various homes of succeeding owners and their descendants, to come to rest finally in the Centennial Museum in Vancouver.

At Macao, Winée decided to return to Hawaii, and was therefore left in the Portuguese city until she could get a place on a ship sailing to the islands. Captain Meares reported taking Winée and Tianna aboard his ship. Tianna was a Hawaiian chief of royal class, about 32 years old, five feet, five inches in stature with "an air of distinction."

Meares wrote:

Our friends of Owyhee had suffered extremely during the passage across the China seas … the poor, unfortunate woman justified our fears concerning her, that she would never again see her friends or native land. She died February 5. At noon her body was committed to the deep; nor was it thought an unbecoming act to grace her remains with the formalities of that religion which opens wide its arms to the whole human race.

Captain Barclay, who commanded the *Imperial Eagle,* was one of those adventurers to the coast of America, who made a very successful voyage. Mrs. Barclay accompanied her husband, and shared with him in the toils, the hardships and vicissitudes incident to such long, as well as perilous voyages; but by no means calculated for the frame, the temper, or the education of the softer sex. This lady was so pleased with the amiable manners of poor Winée that she felt a desire to take her to Europe; and for that purpose took her, with the consent of her friends, under her own particular care and protection. On Mrs. Barclay's departure from China for Europe, Winée was left, as we have already mentioned, in a deep decline, to embark for her country, with the rest of the natives of the Sandwich Islands.

On the morning of her death, she presented Tianna, as a token of her gratitude for his kind attentions to her, with a plate looking-glass, and a bason and bottle of the finest China: to these gifts she also added a gown, a hoop, a petticoat, and a cap for his wife; the rest of her property, consisting of a great variety of articles, she bequeathed to her family; and they were deposited with Tianna, to be delivered to her father and mother.

Nor let fastidious pride cast a smile of contempt on the trifles that composed her little treasure. They were wealth to her and would have given her a very flattering importance, had she lived to have taken them to her native island.[7]

In less than a year, from that fateful day of May 24, 1787, when the white sails of the *Imperial Eagle* appeared on the horizon of her life, Winée had acquired much wealth, which she was fated never to display to her admiring friends and family.

From Canton the *Imperial Eagle* sailed to Mauritius, but it is not known what cargo Charles purchased for delivery at the French island in the Indian Ocean. He and Frances must have felt well pleased with their first year at sea, and certainly the news of their success went round the world. The *Maryland Gazette,* of Baltimore, on August 20, 1790, printed the information that the *Imperial Eagle* left Nootka "with a cargo of near 700 prime sea-otter skins and above 100 of an inferior quality: They had not sold when the *Queen Charlotte* left China, but the price put on them was 30,000 dollars."

However, the Barkleys' joy was short-lived, for they were soon to learn that their partners in the venture had decided to sell the *Imperial Eagle* without just recompense to the captain.

Chapter Five

Mauritius and the End of the First Voyage

hirty thousand dollars was a splendid return on the money invested in ship and men.[1] Unfortunately, as news of the Barkleys' achievement spread through the mercantile world, the success of the enterprise became the very cause of its sudden end, for the Honourable East India Company officials cast jealous eyes upon the upstart company which was making money in the area of their monopoly. The threat of legal action pressured Reid, Beale, Meares and the other merchants into the decision to sell the *Imperial Eagle* and to break their contract with Charles Barkley. The year 1788 would give Frances and Charles their first child but it would deprive them of the *Imperial Eagle*.

From Canton, according to Walbran: "Barkley then made a voyage to Mauritius, returning to Calcutta. Here, owing to injustice and unpleasant treatment at the hands of the ostensible agents of the *Imperial Eagle,* he left his ship, an arbitration board of merchants awarding him £5,000 for the loss of his appointment."[2] Constance Parker's account states that the Barkleys stayed over a year in Mauritius and "received great kindness from the French inhabitants. Her first child was born at Port Louis and was named Hippolite in complement to the kindness received from Monsieur and Madam Collignia. His other names being William and Andrew after his Great Uncles."[3] In Frances' *Reminiscences,* he is "our little William."

Mauritius was not only an important island in the saga of the Barkleys, but also a key factor in the wars and trade of the 18th century. Daring

Portuguese navigators discovered the uninhabited island about 1510, but it was the Dutch, landing in 1598, who named it Mauritius, after Prince Maurice of Nassau. When the sloops returned to the Dutch ships, the sailors brought on board eight or nine great birds and many young ones which they had taken with their hands. Named "dodos" by the Dutch sailors, these strange birds were extinct within a hundred years of their first encounter with Europeans.

To the weary sailors of these centuries, the island must have seemed a paradise, for there were turtles and land tortoises, flowering trees, dodos and rich soil, in which the Dutch planted fruit trees and other plants so that later travellers would find refreshing fruit. Baudelaire has caught the quality of Mauritius in his lines:

> Here is an island in the southern seas;
> I see its harbour full of masts and sails,
> Weary with tossing in the ocean gales.
>
> The sailors' singing, and the scent of trees
> Blossoming o'er the island's hills and dales
> Come to me floating mingled on the breeze.[4]

However, the Dutch, like the Portuguese, sailed away from the island, and it was left to the French, arriving in 1715, to found the first colony in 1722. They named the island Isle de France. Port Louis, their capital, was probably named after Port Louis in Brittany, a harbour from which many French seamen set sail for India. The French desperately needed a safe harbour in the Indian Ocean where ships could shelter from the seasonal cyclones. They began to construct a fortified base, beginning in 1735, whose batteries and walls and docks were only completed about 20 years before the arrival of the *Imperial Eagle*. Port Louis was a well-established French port when the Barkleys stayed there, befriended by the Collignias.

They sailed into Port Louis through a safe channel between Flat Island and Gunner's Quoin (an island with a distinct wedge shape) and saw ahead the jagged peaks of the three mountain chains of the island. The highest peak, the Pence, at 990 metres resembled a thumb held upright. Rising behind Port Louis, Pieter Both is a mountain 870 metres high, with rich green jungle sloping to the coastal plain, where palm trees wave along the shore. By the time of the Barkleys' arrival, Port Louis had already played a vital role in the wars in India, provisioning, repairing and refitting French ships. The collapse of the French empire in India had brought destitution to the island, and the French East India Company was only too happy to sell its rights in Isle de France to the French government.

In 1767 a new era began, when life on the Isle de France was dominated by Pierre Poivre, the intendant and the Vicomte de Souillac, the governor. Poivre, an energetic administrator, promoted agriculture and built mills, a bakery, warehouses, harbour facilities and a press. Port Louis became the headquarters for French travellers and scientists on their way to the Far East, the presence of many distinguished visitors providing an intellectual stimulus. Social life in Port Louis was influenced also by the presence of French refugees from India and by the officers and crews of visiting vessels. Life was a constant succession of festivities, dances and dinner parties, a style of living promoted by the Vicomte de Souillac. When the Barkleys were there, Port Louis had become one of the most attractive ports of call on the route to the East.

As both Frances and Charles enjoyed company, there were probably many happy times at Mauritius. Their good friends the Collignias played an important role at the time of the birth of their first child. It may not have been an easy birth, for one scrap of additional information seems to pertain to this event. Among Constance Parker's papers was a letter from her cousin Ida E. Prosser in British Columbia. Mrs. Prosser first explained that her name before her marriage was Denne, and that her grandfather was Charles Francis Barkley (Frances' son), and then she wrote: "My brother Cecil Denne wrote to me he had seen the Diary of Mrs. Frances Trevor Barkley, and said the account of the birth of twins on one of the small islands with only an Indian woman to care for her, was very pitiful – one of the babies died."[5]

Possibly Frances was left at Mauritius while Charles sailed to Calcutta to settle the fate of the enterprise. Fortunately, Frances' account of the dispute survives in Walbran's "The Cruise of the *Imperial Eagle*":

Upon the arrival of the *Imperial Eagle* in China, Capt. Barkley found the market overstocked with furs, but he managed, after some difficulty, to dispose of his 800 for $30,000 and a cargo was secured for the Mauritius, for which place the *Imperial Eagle* sailed in February 1788. From the Mauritius, the vessel sailed for Calcutta, Capt. Barkley expecting from there to make a second successful voyage to the Northwest coast, but he was disappointed, for on his arrival at Bengal his troubles commenced and terminated, as his wife's diary shows, in his being obliged to give up the command of the vessel, and in addition the persons who compelled him to take this step attempted at the same time to rob him of the large sum he had invested in the venture of the *Imperial Eagle*. Of this interesting subject it will be as well to again quote Mrs. Barkley's Diary.

"The facts are these: My husband was appointed to the command of the *Loudin,* since named the *Imperial Eagle,* and engaged to perform in her three voyages from the East Indies to Japan, Kamskatcha, and the unknown coast of North America, for which he was to have the sum of £3000. His owners were supercargoes in China in the service of the East Indian Company, and several of the owners were directors at home. On my husband's arrival in China, the owners there found they were not warranted in trading to China and the North West coast, even under the Austrian flag, the change being well known and for what purpose. So they found themselves through fear of losing their own situations obliged to sell the ship to avoid worse consequences. They wanted to get off their bargain with my husband, who, having made provision according to the original contract made in London, would have been actually a loser to the sum of thousands of pounds, after making upwards of £10,000 for the owners, since he had been in command, besides the loss of time and great expense incurred by our journey to England from Bengal.

Capt. Barkley, therefore, brought an action for damages, but before the case came into Court at Calcutta, the affair was compromised by an Arbitration of Merchants, and my husband was awarded £5,000. The whole transaction was the most arbitrary assumption of power ever known, for the owners and agents not only dismissed Capt. Barkley from the ship, but appropriated all the fittings and stores laid in by my husband for the term agreed upon, which would have taken at least ten years, for on the second and third voyages he was to winter on the Northwest coast, and with the furs collected trade to the unfrequented parts of China, wherever he thought furs would sell for the highest figure. Of course my husband had supplied himself with the best and most expensive nautical instruments and charts, also stores of every kind for such an adventurous voyage. A great portion of the latter were obliged to be expended for owner's use, who had not laid in sufficient stores for such a voyage, and then these people actually pretended Capt. Barkley was bound to furnish them, and in their first claim, actually brought him apparently in debt to the concern. However, when the contract between Capt. Barkley and the owners was investigated, justice, though to a small extent, prevailed, and he was awarded the sum of £5,000 as I have previously stated. My husband left the vessel with the remaining stores on board, and these articles fraudulently obtained from him were transferred to

John Meares.

Capt. Meares, who was in the same employ, though not ac-
knowledged to be so. In the same manner as he got the stores,
Capt. Meares got possession of my husband's journal and plans
from the persons in China to whom he was bound under a
penalty of £5,000 to give them up for a certain time, for, as these
persons stated, mercantile objects, they not wishing the knowledge of the Coast to be published.

Capt. Meares, however, with the greatest effrontery, published
and claimed the merit of my husband's discoveries therein contained, besides inventing lies of the most revolting nature tending
to vilify the person he thus pilfered. No cause could be assigned,
either by Capt. Barkley or myself for this animosity, except the
wish of currying favour with late agents and owners of the
Loudin, named the *Imperial Eagle*, these persons having quar-
relled with Captain Barkley in consequence of his claiming on
his discharge a just demand."

This terminated the connection of Capt. Wm. Barkley and his
wife with the *Imperial Eagle*.[6]

Frances' voice was not the first nor the strongest to accuse Meares of
lying and stealing. Captain Robert Haswell, in his log of the voyage of the
American vessels *Columbia* and *Washington* in 1788 wrote: "Capt. Meares
protested that both vessells [*Felice* and *Iphigenia*, Meares' vessels] ever since
they had been on the coast had not collected fifty skins; on our smileing
(for we had been differently informed) he said it was a fact upon his sacred
word of honour, so intent was this Gentleman in deceiving us that he
hesitated not to forfeit his word and Honour to what we were convinced
was a notorious falsity."[7] Meares alleged that he had purchased land at
Friendly Cove from Maquinna, but Captain Joseph Ingraham's manuscript
journal asserts that, in September of 1792, Maquinna made a declaration
that he had never sold any lands whatsoever to Mr. Meares. Moreover,
Maquinna, according to Mozino, called Meares "Aita-aita Meares" which
means "the lying Meares." In his own account of his voyages, Meares related that Duncan, captain of the *Princess Royal*, another King George's
Sound Company vessel, complained to him of bad treatment received from
Captain Dixon, but Duncan subsequently wrote a letter in which he denied

that he had made such a statement, and Dixon in 1790 published a statement of assistance given to Captain Duncan.[8]

Captain George Dixon's is the loudest voice to condemn Meares. In his scathing document *Remarks on the Voyages of John Meares, Esq. in a letter to that gentleman,* printed for the author and sold by John Stockdale, Piccadilly, and George Goulding, James Street, Covent Garden, in 1790, he began by calling Meares' book "scarcely anything more than a confused heap of contradictions and misrepresentations."[9] Meares had written that Dixon's voyages in the *King George* and *Queen Charlotte* had accomplished little either in commerce or discovery. Dixon answered this by challenging Meares to take the trouble to compare Dixon's chart with any former ones and stated that a copy of his (Dixon's) chart "was given to you I believe by John Henry Cox, Esq. of Canton, some time before you sailed for the coast of America; at the same time he gave you a copy of Captain Barclays chart from Nootka Sound to the Southward along the coast, as far, or nearly so, as you went; together with a chart of the coast, or at least that part of it which Don Francisco Maurelle had touched at, and all the information that could be obtained from Captains Hannah, Lowrie and Guise." Dixon asked, "Why not say at once to your associate, 'I was favoured by Mr. Cox with an account of this place, together with a copy of a chart which Captain Dixon gave him in China'? This would have been telling the plain trouth at once; but this I presume did not suit your purpose; palpable falsehood, or studied misrepresentations seem to be the most striking traits of your very extraordinary performance."[10]

In proof of the commercial success of his voyage, Dixon printed the following interesting tally:[11]

Captain Hanna, first voyage	560	sea-otter skins
" second voyage	100	"
And of slips and pieces 300 sold as	60	"
Captains Lowrie and Guise	604	"
Captain Meares, first voyage	357	"
Captain Barclay	800	"
	2481	
Captains Portlock and Dixon	2552	"

Referring specifically to Captain Barkley's chart, Dixon gave the positions of different places on the coast as carefully recorded by Barkley:

Lat.	North	Long.	West of Greenwich	
47	9	125	23	Point Fear
47	43	125	1	Destruction River
47	47	125	14	Pinnacle
48	8	125	31	Cape Flattery
48	24	125	47	Center of Tallock Island
48	26	125	44	South point of De Fear's entrance
48	33	125	48	North point ditto
48	50	126	00	South point Barclay's Sound
49	00	126	17	West point ditto
		127	0	West point Nootka[12]

Dixon then commented, in his published letter to Meares, "Whether or not this chart has been of service to you, the most superficial reader of your voyage will be able to discover; but your gratitude seems to keep pace with your other intellectual endowments, as I do not find in the whole course of your work, the smallest acknowledgement made for the many advantages you derived from it."[13]

After a careful review of the evidence, Judge Howay could find no contemporary contradiction of any of George Dixon's statements "or the least suggestion that Dixon was not a man of honour and of scrupulous accuracy." He finished his study of the Dixon-Meares controversy with this statement:

The conclusion of the whole matter so far as Meares is concerned is that he endeavoured to magnify his own explorations at the expense of his predecessors; that he made many statements, important and unimportant, without any knowledge of the facts, with a reckless disregard of the truth, or with knowledge of their untruth; that in the discussion of the price of sea-otter skins (which was to him the subject of importance) he has omitted material factors, falsified documents, and made knowingly untrue statements; and that, in consequence, he is not entitled to have credence placed on his unsupported testimony. This opinion has been shown to be in accord with that of his contemporaries.[14]

The truth of Meares' deception can be seen in his own published account of his voyages. As he was sailing south from Nootka, following Barkley's route (and using Barkley's chart), Meares wrote, "We knew of no other navigator said to have been this way, except Maurelle; and his chart, which we now had on board, convinced us that he had either never seen this part of the coast, or that he had purposely misrepresented it:"[15] Meares then arrived at the Strait of Juan de Fuca, and without mentioning Barkley's rediscovery of the passage a year earlier, wrote "this strait, which we shall call by the name of its original discoverer, John de Fuca ..."[16] In another part of his book, Meares contradicts an earlier statement ("no other navigator said to have been this way") by referring to "the great bay or sound which we had passed the day after our departure from Port Cox [Tofino] and from whence a large company of natives came off to us. This bay had, indeed, been already visited by the ship *Imperial Eagle*, where we had found a secure anchorage."[17] Meares observed "the Easternmost head-land of the large sound near Port Cox, which obtained from us the name of Cape Beale;"[18] Frances had recorded, a year before Meares saw it, the naming of Cape Beale after the purser of the *Imperial Eagle*.

It therefore appears that Frances Barkley's accusations are supported by evidence from her contemporaries, and that Dixon's final remarks to Meares are entirely justified:

> Whatever may be your abilities, it was surely in your power, (wherever you have found your own inexperience aided by the information of others) to acknowledge from what sources you derived your information; or, if they fortunately succeeded in making any interesting discoveries, or throwing new lights on the branch of commerce in which you were engaged, you surely might have left them enjoy their hard earned portion of merit in quiet, and not have endeavoured, by detracting from others, to add to your own. But no, this you could not possibly do; and therefore a spirit of envious detraction, and fastidious misrepresentation, is

met with almost in every page of your work. I could not therefore suffer it to be ushered into the world unnoticed.[19]

Thus Frances and Charles Barkley found themselves defrauded by Meares and the other merchants, deprived of the *Imperial Eagle* and stranded in Mauritius, with their lives complicated by the presence of the infant William Hippolyte Andrew. Constance Parker wrote about their return to England, giving a quotation from the lost Diary. They left Mauritius, she states, in an American ship:

> ... commanded by a Capt. Babcock, who bore a brutal character. They sailed round the Cape of Good Hope, up the coast of Africa, passed Spain etc. and almost in sight of England were wrecked off the Banque de l'Edain, the Bay of Havre, owing to the bad man-agement of the Captain. The ship's bottom was beaten in but her cargo being cotton kept her afloat and with the assistance of every boat in the Harbour she was towed into Harfleur where she foundered and was lost. The Diary says: "My beloved husband, myself and one infant son, a pupil of my husband's and two faithful followers found ourselves alone on the wreck the morning of the night she struck, the vile Captain and his crew having deserted us and the ship in the night." A few days later they embarked on an English packet and arrived at Portsmouth 12th November 1789. Mrs. Barkley was then only 20 1/2 years old. No word of grumbling is heard at the countless hardships and dangers tho' the food consisted of salt pork and rice for months at a time.[20]

The Barkleys had sailed from Ostend on November 24, 1787; their re-turn to Portsmouth was almost precisely two years later, on November 12, 1789. No account survives of the joyous reunions and the visiting.

Chapter Six
India: The Second Voyage Begins

s Charles had given up a secure position with the East India Company to become involved in the Bengal Fur Company enterprise, hoping to acquire great wealth in the venture, the collapse of the ten-year scheme undoubtedly left Charles and Frances uncertain concerning their future. In the circumstances, they decided to return to India, which had provided fortunes for many other energetic young British gentlemen. Charles was given the command of the ship *Princess Frederica* and after some delays the second voyage began.

This journey would be eventful for the Barkleys. Frances would give birth to a baby girl just as they were rounding the Cape of Good Hope and struggling against gale-force winds. Running short of provisions they would stop for a week at Mauritius, stocking up on stores and visiting old friends. Upon leaving Mauritius the Barkleys would face the most dangerous leg of the journey, sailing along the infamous Malabar Coast with its stormy seas, teeming rainfall, poor visibility and risk of attack from French privateers. On August 22, 1791, after having weathered 11 months at sea, Captain Barkley would bring the *Princess Frederica* into Calcutta. This was to be their final voyage; Calcutta would be home and where they would seek their fortunes, or so they planned.

Under the heading "II Voyage," Constance Parker wrote:

After resting seven months in England, my great Grand

Parents started on another voyage in a large ship 1200 ton and built of Indian teak wood. Capt. Barkley was in command but had only a part share in her. The ship was at Elsinore where they had to join her, and owing to many delays they had to remain the summer in Copenhagen, but met Mrs. Barkley's sister there. Finally, they started the early part of 1791, bound for the Royal Dockyard, Bombay, leaving [taking] their little son with them. The second child Martha was born during a violent gale off Cape Horn. They approached the Coast near Bombay in June, but the winds prevented their landing and they were driven down the coast, unable to effect a landing and had to sail round Cape Comorin and try to deliver the cargo at Madras. This entailed a heavy loss. From Madras they went to Calcutta.[1]

Confirming some details from the Constance Parker account, there is a letter in the East India Company archives dated April 27, 1792, from Fort William (Calcutta) and addressed "To the Secret Committee of the Honourable Court of Directors." The letter includes these statements:

> The ship *Princess Frederica,* Captain Barclay, left Copenhagen on the 8th of Oct. 1790 and arrived here the latter end of August last. She touched at Madras on her passage hither and landed there near 1,500 bars of iron and a few articles of liquor etc. No mention is made in her manifest of military stores imported at this Presidency.[2]

It seems that the secret committee was looking for smuggled weapons.

Although it is uncertain whether the *Princess Frederica* left Copenhagen in October of 1790, as the East India Company letter states, or early in 1791, further details of this voyage are well established, as part of the log survives. The first entry is dated Sunday, May 8, 1791, after the ship had weathered the violent gale off the Cape of Good Hope, during which the baby Martha (Patty) had been born, and now sailed with "light airs and fair weather."

Giving birth on a sailing ship was a challenging prospect. As there were passengers aboard there probably were a number of women who could come to Frances' aid. Normally she would expect her husband to help in the delivery; it was common practice for the captain to take care of all emergency medical duties, including midwifery. However, as they were dealing with gale-force winds, Charles would most likely have been on deck tending to the safety of his ship. In any case, Frances would have been buffeted about the cabin as the ship battled the steep seas and high winds. Fortunately they were only a week away from friends and respite in the Mauritius. Caring for a babe in arms was difficult at best, but aboard ship, any problems or emergencies would be almost insurmountable. They were obviously low on food and as Frances took her baby to her breast she knew that she would need to produce a plentiful flow of milk for without it, her daughter would weaken and die. If a ship did not have any nanny goats some mothers, finding themselves unable to nurse, would turn to rice water sweetened with sugar in an attempt to provide nourishment for their babies. In rough weather Frances would need to secure herself and Patty to keep from being tossed about; she might have sewed the baby into her bed or crib by binding the swaddling blanket to the mattress. Nothing would be easy in this environment: even washing diapers presented a challenge. Fresh water was always at a premium so washing in saltwater would be the norm. Salt-encrusted diapers would have caused boils and open sores which do not heal easily, and infection often followed. Frances writes of none of this in her *Reminiscences*.

A week in Mauritius would be a welcome respite. However, the storms apparently delayed the ship, for on Sunday, May 29, the entry in the log noted: "This day served out the last of the Ship's bread that is eatable except about 50 lb." On the day following, the log recorded the details of the approach to Mauritius, where they moored on June 4. The fresh bread baked at Port Louis must have tasted like manna, and Frances and Charles were probably delighted to renew the friendships and to visit the Collignias once more, but the log noted only the ship's business:

Tuesday, June 7, 1791: "Employed getting our Guns up out of the hold and mounting them, getting ready to receive our Water. Peter Martin Seaman claimed the protection of his Flag as a Frenchman and was discharged."

Wednesday, June 8: "Light breezes off the land and fair weather. Andrea Nicholitz, Manuel Francisco and Matthew

Frenwick were sent in confinement aboard the *Medusa,* Frigate, for Mutiny."

Thursday, June 9: "Rec'd on board bread, arrack ... one cask white wine for the ship and one for the Captain ... 18 ducks, 66 Fowl, 6 Turkies, 6 Hogs, 4 Goats ... some plantains, potatoes, yarns, sweet potatoes, pumkins, Indian corn, onions." [The three men that were sent on board the frigate were discharged.] "Rec'd on board 21 cases wine."

Sunday, June 12: "Rec'd on board some Hay and some live stock. Hoisted in the Long Boat and Yawl. The pilot came on board. Weighed the Bower anchors and winded the ship. Got everything ready for Sea. Rec'd some furniture belonging to Capt. Barkley."

The week of visiting was over and Frances and the two children were back on board the ship, but the *Princess Frederica* waited for a fair wind:

Monday, June 13: "Winds were light in the morning and in the evening too calm to get under sail, which is the reason we do not sail. Everybody being on board, got the Top Gallant Yards up."

Tuesday, June 14: "Winds chiefly light and variable with fine weather in the morning. Everybody on board waiting for the land wind to get under sail."

Wednesday, June 15: "Fresh springing up at 2 PM. Slipped the moorings and sailed out of Port Louis. At 1/2 past 2 PM the pilot left us. Saluted the land and Commodore each with 9 Guns which was returned with Equal Number."

Sunday, June 19: "Fresh gales and a short uneasy sea. Great flocks of boobies[3] and sea pigeons."

Tuesday, July 5: "Thick weather and squally. The sea the first part of the night appearing so luminous as to reflect a shadow of the ship and appearing one White Foam ... Kept a good lookout in the forenoon for land. Very thick. Could not see more than 1 Mile. A prodigious sea from the North."

Wednesday, July 6: "Blowing very hard with Constant Squalls and rain so thick could not see a Mile. When it cleared a little we stood in and at 1/2 past 6 PM saw land which I take to be Mallabar Point, the lighthouse on Old Woman's Island and which I was confirmed in by seeing the light at night. It came on Very thick and Squally and being in 12 fathom Water could only clear the land by Standing to the Southward. Tacked at 2 AM in hopes of getting near by in the Morning. At Daylight it being a little clear so that we could see three or four miles, stood in to 13 fathom when it came on again to Blow & so thick could not see one mile. Was obliged to stand to the South again to clear the shore. The sea immensely high."

Although thousands of ships approached the Malabar Coast from early September through April, sailing along it in July was extremely hazardous. Ships would run afoul of the southwest monsoon with its lashing rain, strong winds and confused seas. Local shipping was generally laid up from the end of May until the beginning of September as insurers would not risk payment to ships or cargo lost during the monsoon season. However, the monsoons were not the only concern along this coast.

There were increasing incidents of sea battles, piracy and highjacking, and the British navy was unable to protect their ships from pirates and French privateers. The French frigates out-sailed and out-gunned the slow, lumbering trade ships, so for protection, many British ships travelled in convoy. In the back of every master's mind was the fear of boarding or capture, because they were well aware of treatment they would receive at the hands of these mercenaries. Ships were pillaged, crew were brutalized, and there were many stories of captains being dragged around the deck of their ship, while pirates repeatedly stabbed them with their poniards. Fortunately the Barkleys sailed unnoticed and had only to contend with the tempestuous seas.

The log continues:

Thursday, July 7: "In the evening at 1/2 past 3 saw the high land again. Immediately stood in to make it but it soon was hid again though not more than 2 leagues Distance. The barometer suddenly fell an Inch. The ship in 14 fathom. No possibility of standing to the Northward. Stood again to the South. The wind being N could not think of standing to the North, the sea being so immensely high. We called a consultation wherein it was the

General Opinion that to attempt getting to the Northward would be attended with great Danger to the Ship, and that if a Gale of Wind came on we might not be able to keep off the Coast. Very little hopes of the Wind favoring us as to reach Bombay and being very short of Provisions we determined for the General good to get clear of the Coast as soon as possible and seek a Port to Eastward. Having no Provisions to enable us to attempt the southern passage back again therefore make the [undecipherable] of our way to procure [incomplete]."

Sunday, July 10: "Moderate gales. The Sea in the Night had a very luminous appearance and alarmed us at first, looking like breakers. Lost our lead and 25 fathoms of line."[4]

Saturday, July 23: "At noon in sight of Madrass Road."

Sunday, July 24: "At 3 anchored to the South of all the Shipping with the Best Bower in 9 fathoms. At daylight weighed and run into a good berth. The passengers went on shore. Found riding here several of the Honorable East India Company ships and five ships of war. The *Phoenix, Minerva, Thames, Ariel.* Rec'd on board fresh Provisions for the Ship's Company. This log ends at midnight."

Nothing is written of the wonderful solidness of land under the feet of the passengers, nor of the easing of tensions after the gale-blown passage; nor is there any mention of how Frances cared for an infant and a small boy in such perilous circumstances. After several blank pages, the log continues:

Saturday, August 13: "Rec'd on board from the Master Attend-ant an anchor weighing 18 CWT 11 lbs. with stock and all com-plete, which is paid for in bills on the Owners. Against Barrett Esq. of Calcutta. At 3 AM. the land wind came off. Weighed and came to sail. Stood out to get an offing till 8 AM."

Sunday, August 22: "Moored near Calcutta."

From Constance Parker it is known that at Calcutta

for a time they had comfort staying with Mr. and Mrs. Forbes. Mrs. Forbes was Capt. Barkley's great Aunt (nee Ann Barkley) and Mr.

Forbes, who was a big merchant in Calcutta, was a Forbes of Cromarty, and Captain Barkley was a great favourite of both of them. Mrs. Forbes stood godmother to the second child Patty. The Barkleys now wished to settle down there [in Calcutta] to trade in the country as the sea faring life had not brought prosperity. The diary continues "My beloved husband furnished a handsome house intending to settle down and trade, but our evil star brought his elder brother Capt. John Barkley to Calcutta in command of the *Lord Hawksbury* and he set his face against the trading as derogatory — and managed to fit out an Expedition to the N.W. coast of America of 2 sailing vessels, the *Halcyon* and the *Venus* and insisting on his brother taking command of the *Halcyon,* a brig of 60 tons". They tried to prevail on Mrs. Barkley to remain in Calcutta "tempting me with a fair garden and house on the banks of the Hooghly, but I preferred all dangers of the sea with peace of mind and my dear Husband as comfort to all the [indecipherable] of the East, but from that day I date all our misfortunes."[5]

For Charles, the arrival at Calcutta was a homecoming, for he had grown up in the humid Anglo-Indian city. Many times he must have observed how the vivid blue waters of the Bay of Bengal turned gradually violet and then a dark brown as one approached the delta of the great rivers, nearing Calcutta, and how the pungent odours drifted out to sea to greet the sailors on deck

East side of the river at Calcutta, from Views of Calcutta, 1786, by *Thomas Daniell. Drawn by J. F. Whittingham.*

long before they could see the low coast, which merged with the horizon in a haze of August heat. Then the sea became a muddy yellow and wind-blown coconut trees could be seen along the shore. As the ship entered the Hooghly River, the jungle closed in on either bank, asleep in the oppressive, late-afternoon heat. Ships moved slowly up the muddy river, the small fishing boats gliding out of the way.

Only a century before, the city had not existed at all, for Calcutta is one of the youngest of the world's great cities. In 1690 Job Charnock, a member of the East India Company, had pitched his tents on the site of Calcutta and so founded the city. Kipling penned some verse on the subject:

> Thus the midday halt of Charnock — more's the pity! —
> Grew a city.
> As the fungus sprouts chaotic from its bed
> So it spread.
> Chance-directed, chance-erected, laid and built
> On the silt,
> Palace, byre, hovel — poverty and pride
> Side by side,
> And above the packed and pestilential town
> Death looked down.[6]

It would be difficult to imagine a worse place for a city. Calcutta sits sodden on the delta of the Ganges and the Brahmaputra Rivers, the Hooghly being a distributary of the Ganges. Warm even in winter, by mid-March the heat is searing, and before the monsoons come the temperature can be as high as 43°C. Tensions build until the monsoons break in June, with crashing thunder and sheets of rain. When the rain stops, the city steams. Torrential rain and hot steam alternate for four months. The whole area of the delta is a tropical fen, a perfect breeding place for mosquitoes, but on this tropical bog, the British built the city. By the time of Warren Hastings' return to Calcutta as governor in 1772, mansions and fine stone buildings had been constructed and the Anglo-Indian lifestyle was flourishing.

Some idea of the scene when Charles and Frances decided to buy a house in Calcutta may be derived from Geoffrey Moorhouse's description of an elegant ball which revolved for a night around the exquisite Miss Sanderson, who so captivated the rich young men of Calcutta that 16 of them turned up simultaneously wearing a livery modelled on her pea-green French frock with pink silk trimmings: "the lovely object ... ready to expire with heat ... with a muslin handkerchief in each hand, employed in the delightful office of wiping down her face while the big drops stand impearled upon her forehead."[7] In the Calcutta of that day men outnumbered women, and many an English girl made the long, tedious journey by sailing ship in the hope of finding a husband; if she got someone in the growing civil service it meant an income of £300 and a pension when he died. Sunday morning on the church steps became the great place for examining new arrivals. It was an introverted, isolated, corrupt society. The palanquin was the only method of travel; the passenger reclined on cushions inside while four bearers staggered along rough jungle trails. Even inside the area of the city, marauding tigers and footpads were dangerous at night, and the malarial mosquito was ever present.

Although there were a few wealthy Bengalis of the upper class, for the most part the British regarded the natives as servants, of which each household had a swarm. Thirty to forty servants per household was common and one family of four had one hundred and ten.[8] The British had not achieved this position of dominance without a struggle. At first the East India Company had only asked the native rulers for permission to establish trading posts, but gradually the company grew from the status of a group of merchant traders to a great administrative power, controlling vast revenues, maintaining an army,

A street scene in Calcutta, 1786.

waging war. The Regulating Act of 1773, the first step toward Crown control of India, elevated Warren Hastings to the rank of governor-general of all India. The British justified their presence with the argument that Indian culture had been corrupted by a false religion and could only be transformed by the introduction of Christianity.

The period from 1786 to 1805, when Charles and Frances decided to live in Calcutta, can be called the Golden Age of the British in India, when military conquests had given them control of wide territories and great wealth. Wages for company servants were low, but the officers were allowed to do some trading on their own account and grew wealthy from bribes and gifts. English merchants in India were permitted to carry on a private trade, under licence from the East India Company, called the "country trade." Pepper and raw cotton were carried to China, and tea and Chinese goods brought to India for sale to other merchants whose ships carried the goods to Europe and the rest of the world. It was this very profitable "country trade" which Charles and Frances had decided to undertake, until Charles' older brother John arrived and disapproved of the scheme. Of this crisis in their lives, Frances wrote a detailed account.

Her *Reminiscences* contain only a few pages about the first voyage, the cruise of the *Imperial Eagle,* and throughout those pages she left many blank spaces where her memory failed. The account of the second voyage, in the *Halcyon,* is quite different. It has a firm, sure style and is detailed and precise, probably based on her Diary, which she referred to as "some old papers" and in which she found "the substance of these remarks, made at the time." Now when she left a blank space she promised to continue "when I can find any data."

For five months the Barkleys enjoyed the life and leisure of Calcutta before they set sail for the northwest coast of North America. The circumstances of this trip were not at all to their liking. Both Charles and Frances were reluctant to venture forth on yet another sea voyage, especially with a baby and young child in tow. But Charles' older brother John was most insistent that the life in the country trade was not suitable for a former East India Company man. He persuaded Charles to partner a joint venture expedition taking sugar and arrack, a distilled drink made from rice, sugar, or the sap of palm, to Kamchatka where he would purchase sea otter pelts for the China trade. The ship that would carry Frances and her growing family was a tiny,

80-ton brig, a two-masted square-rigged vessel that was considerably inferior to what they were used to. There was not much room for attending to the necessities of growing children, their living quarters were cramped, and in general Frances and the children would be restricted in their movements. This was not going to be a comfortable trip, but with her usual equanimity, Frances complained little and made the most of the situation.

Using the Diary as source, she wrote:

1791 Second Voyage

Left Calcutta in Bengal on the 29th of December 1791 on board the Brigg *Halcion* bound to the North West Coast of America, in Company with the Cutter *Venus,* these two Vessels having been bought and fitted for the Voyage to the South Seas at the joint expense of Captn. Barkley, and Mr. Lambart of Calcutta, a Merchant in the firm of Lambart & Ross. The expedition was intended to extend to Kamschatca & Japan and a Cargo consisting of Sugar, Arrac and other produce of Mr. Lambarts Factory and Farm at a place on the Banks of the Hooghly River called Mayapoor, a little below Achepoor. We landed at this place, and were much interested with the country, and the curious scenes that were presented to our view. Mr. Lambert has built a very neat House, his Manager a Mr. Scott, who resides in it, and conducts the Manufactory. The house is finely situated on the River, and commands on it a very extensive View. Ships bound either up or down the River sail very near the Banks, but at the back of the settlement the jungle seround and inclose it, and it is no comfortable sensation at Night to know that you are liable to the Visits of the Wild Beasts, prinsipally Tigars. We did not see any, but saw & were sadly anoy'd by the Noise of troops of Jackalls, a sort of Wild Dog which is very troublesome.

The Sugar is Manufactured entirely by Chinese Who have been brought here by Mr. Lambart and regularly settled in a Village built according to the Chinese taste, where they live on the Estate by themselves according to their own Customs, and are very orderly and diligent. The Sugar made on this estate is particularly fine.

Three Ships have loaded and sailed from hence bound to Europe this year with entire Cargoes from the Estate, consisting of Sugar Rum, which is in great estimation, and Arrac, and great hopes are entertained of this New branch of trade from Bengal, and when better understood, will furnish imployment for the Natives, as the Sugar Cane can be produced in any quantity when labour is so cheap. The site of the Plantation is particularly well chosen, as there is a Creek Runs through the Estate convenient for shipping off the Merchandise. The Ships that have hitherto sailed from hence are bound to Ostend in Flanders and it is said that notwithstanding the distance, Sugar can be landed from hence to Europe cheaper than from the West India Islands. After two days of pleasure on shore, we felt very loath to leave this peaceful spot, where every department was conducted with the utmost regularity, to imbark on board a Vessel inferior in all respects to what I had been accostomed too. However, the liberal supply of Vegetables sent on board by our good Friend Mr. Scott, we were often put in mind of his friendship. Some very fine Cabbages in Pots gave us much pleasure, as they grew and flourished amazingly on board, and the sight of them was quite a treat, which none but mariners can appreciate.

To them any verdure is grateful to the Eye, and during our passage down this Magnificent River we tryed to forget the ease & comfort we left behind, and our presentiments of Evil were but to well verefied in the sequal, for from the date of this unadvised Expedition all our misfortunes took their rise, and are all attributable to the advice and fatal Influance of our Evil Genius Captn. John Barkley, whom our unlucky star brought to Calcutta just in time to frustrate all our plans which were to settle in Calcutta, where my poor dear Husband had taken, and partly furnished a very Comfortable House, landed his investment out of the *Princess Fridarica*, consisting of sheet Copper and Marine stores intended for Bombay, a quantity of Plait Glass, and ornamental articles, and a large stock of Cologne Gin, all of which would no doubt have sold well, in the course of time, altho at the time the Markets were very low; but as his intention was to imbark in what is termed the country service, that is to say to trade from Port to Port in India. For the Command of a Ship in such a service he was emmenantly qualefied, and with the advice of Mr. Forbs, a Cousin of his, everything was put in train for the prosicution of this plan, nothing but patience required; but of that, Alas, he was deficient. He began to dispair of selling his Cargo, and to get alarmed at the expenses of our Establishment, and just in the nick of time his Brother arrived in the Command of the *Lord Hawksbury,* Indiaman. This Brother of his began by disapproving of everything and painting his Brother's situation in the most gloomy colours, alarmed his fears & ultimately succeeded in persuading him that it was very derogatory in him to become a Country Captn. which at that time was not considered a genteel line of Life, altho large fortunes have since been made in it. Mr. Forbes, who had previously forwarded his views, now became cool upon it, and to cut the matter short, my husband gave up a plan, which but for the Pride of his Brother, would probably have made him a large fortune; for it was a great matter, in those days, to begin with a capital which he had at that time realised to the amount of four thousand pound, and had at that moment in unperishable goods in his House. But want of patience in him & the pride of his Brother led to very fatal results.

At this juncture of Affairs, his late Voyages began to be much talked of, and a Gentleman of the Name of Connolly, at that time a lewtenant in the Navy, was Chief Mate on board the *Lord Hawksbury* and an old friend of both Brothers, being a well informed Man and having conexions in the Mercantile line, suggested the advantages of making another Voyage to the Pacific Ocian, and a Friend of his, a Mr. Lambart, the Gentleman before aluded to, made Captn. Barkley proposals, and the voyage which was now under my consideration was undertaken: two paltry vessels bought at a great cost, the one a Brig of Eighty Tons burden (the *Halcion*) and a still smaller, the *Venus,* both to sail a certain distance together, then to seperate. The *Venus,* who by the bye was commanded by a great Rascal, was to go to the North West Coast of America and the *Halcion* to Kamchatca, the Kurile Islands and Japan, and afterward to join Company in Nootka Sound.

Clothing list for the voyage of the Halcyon, *written by Frances Barkley in Calcutta, 1791.*

For this wise scheme, the House, Furniture, all our little valuables; this Ships Cargo &&c were left to the mercy of strangers, and in less than three Months we were again imbarked on board a small Vessel indifferently Officered, and worse Manned, the sailors being chiefly Lascars unused to Cold climates or the dangers and difficulties to be anticipated in such an Undertaking. With this Crew we were once more doomed to circumnavigate the Globe. It is but justice however to my dear Husband and his pretended friends to acknowlidge that I had my option of remaining in Bengal, and it was planned by the latter, and reluctantly agreed to by the former, that I should be left under the Care of Mr. Lambart and to reside at his Garden House, a beautiful Bungaloo on the Banks of the Rivar, in Garden Reach, where I was to have Servants, Palanqueens and every Luxery, which were painted in the most glowing colours by Captn. John, who did not appear to think there was any impropriety in my accepting.

His Brother was to return in less than a twelve month, and we were to be set up in grand style. He succeeded in persuading his Brother that it would be madness in him to take me with him with two Children, which was all true enough. But I considered the alternative worse, for Young and inexperienced as I was I could not overlook the impropriety of the plan, and in spight of the sneers of Mrs. Forbs, who patronised it and thought me very squeamish in rejecting, I resolutely insisted upon declining, much to the satisfaction of My Husband, who never thought of being seperated from me; but when he became sensible of the great inconveniances he was subjecting me too, he began to waver, and when to late saw his error in entering into a speculation so detrimental to our comfort & happiness. Blinded by the Spirit of Enterprise, he never weighed sufficiantly the differance between the Brigg *Halcion* and the Ship *Louden,* in which we had been so comfortable, so that when it came to the push and he felt the difficultys he actually agreed to leave me; but united as we were in affection, I dont think he would have persevered even if I had given in to the plan. Therefore I relieved him of his anxieties by making it appear to be my whim. In fact it was so, for when I

saw that it was in vain to resist the scheme, which I did as long
as I could venture, I made up my mind to brave every danger
rather than seperate, thereby at any rate securing his peace of
Mind, as well as my own; but we both imbarked with heavy
hearts, two Infants to share all risks, the Youngest at the breast.
She, poor little creature, became the Victim of our folly. But I
must return to my former subject —

I have been led into this digreshion by the perusal of some old
papers I had to refer too for dates, when I unexpectedly found the
Substance of these remarks, made at the time.

To proceed then on our unpromising Voyage begun under
every disadvantage, for we were too late for the regular Trade
Wind, which obliged Captn. Barkley to try a very unusual and
unfrequented Track between the Sooloo Archipilego of Islands. In
the Straits of Macassar we were becalmed three Weeks, but I
should have first mentioned in pursuance of my Introduction to
this unlucky Voyage, that shortly after we left Mayapoor, we got
down the River below Diamond Harbour and the next day to
Cox's Island, where we found the *Phoenix,* Indiaman, lying, bound
to Calcutta. She was commanded by Captn. Gray, who kindly
took our Pilot back, and was instrumental with Mr. Terry the
deputy Master attendent, in procuring us a Boat belonging to one
of the Pilot Schooners at this station, which was a great accommodation, Captn. B. having left Calcutta without one, depending on
one promised him by his Brother out of the *Lord Hawksbury* then
lying ready to Sail homeward bound, at Diamond Harbour; in
which he was disappointed by the negligance of Capn. John, who
never forwarded any orders to the Officer in charge, so that but
for this lucky encounter, we might have gone to sea without our
compliment of Boats; very Brotherly conduct.

The Pilot left us on the Evening of the 6th of January 1792,
and we thought to get clear off, but the Wind changing we were
obliged to Anchor that Night, as were the Indiamen, which gave
Captn. B. an opportunity of taking leave of his kind friend Capt.
Gray, who loaded [him] with kindness, and good wishes and
furnished him with every kind of information he could collect. In

fact, he took the greatest interest in the Voyage, which in so
small a Vessel seemed to everyone a most dangerous undertaking.
Notwithstanding which, Captn. Gray complimented his Friend
by saying that if *talents, prudence* and good sailorship could
ensure success, he would ensure it. This sort of encouragement
from a Man whose judgement was good could not fail of pro-
ducing its Effects, and accordingly, he returned in good spirits,
and the next morning the 7th of January we made sail and soon
parted company with the other Ships and took a last farewell of
the shores of Bengal.

The Weather was so fine that the Vessel had scearce any
Motion, and we began to think we should not find so much
inconvenience from the smallness of the Vessel as we had anticipated and we were all in high spirits. We were, however, soon
convinced of our error, for in the course of the Night a high Wind
arose and the boisterous waves soon set our poor little Bark in
motion. The Rain fell in torrents and the poor Lascars were soon
driven below, almost drowned.

The British merchant fleet had expanded so rapidly that it had out-
grown its supply of seamen. As a result, regulations were relaxed to allow for
three-fifths of the crew to be made up of foreign seamen. The use of Lascars,
Indian sailors, became common. Lascars were said to be hard-working and
obedient but could not be depended upon in a crisis. Accustomed to a tem-
perate climate they suffered considerably in cold weather. They were treated
badly and fed a steady diet consisting mostly of rice; consequently they quite
readily died of scurvy and malnutrition.

The Wind blew a hurican and wafted us in Ten days, during
which time it blew a gale to the entrance of the Straits of Sunda.
This kind of Weather is very uncommon at this Season, and therefore appeared worse than it was in reality, besides being unused to
the quick motion of so small a Vessel, besides the having a smaller
Vessel in View. The *Venus,* which is a very beautiful little Vessel,
appeared compleatly the sport of the Waves, tumbling and tossing
about at a strange rate, sometimes buried in a gulph and hid from

our sight in the trough of the Sea and then emerging from the breakers that seemed every moment to overwhelm her so that we fancied at times we saw her keel out of the water as she turned over from the deep trough of the sea upon the swelling waves. To add to our discomfort the weather was intensily hot, nothwithstanding which we were obliged to the necessity of shutting all the Ports so that we could not get a breath of Air without exposing ourselves to the torrents of Rain upon deck. The poor dear Children were almost sofocated, but fortunately not sick, and my anxiety for them kept me from giving way, for the whole care and fatigue of attending to them entirely devolved on me, our two black Girls being compleatly knocked up with sea sickness and fright.

This boisterous weather was succeeded by a fine Breeze and fair weather, and on the 25th of January at daylight we made the Island of Ingano, which is off the entrance of the Straits. We passed this Island at a distance of four leagues and so saw but little of it. It is inhabited by Malays and has a fine harbour to Leeward. In the Evening we discry'd Mount Pogong on the Coast of Sumatra, and at daylight on the 26th after lying too some hours, made the low land about flat Point, and afterwards cast Anchor between the Island of Kakatoire and Tamorand Island. On the 27th weighed Anchor and stood into the Bay on the Coast of the Island of Kakatoire, to take in Wood and fill up the Water casks & &c. The island is high and covered with Trees of differant kinds, some emensely large, and there is a small Village of Malays at the watering place. The number of Inhabitants does not exceed an hundred. They brought plenty of Turtle, plantin's, Mangoes, Cocoa Nutts, pumkins and Musk Melons, and a few Water Melons. I went on Shore often, but was not allowed to stray far inland as the Malays are not to be trusted. We frequently landed on the small Islands in the Bay to take a strole, and found ripe Mangoes on the trees, which were very acceptable, as what were brought on board were all unripe.

We remained in this Anchorage until the 3d of February. The day before we Sailed from thence, we experienced a dreadful thunderstorm. One clap of thunder laid us all prostrate on the Deck, but did us no other damage. The *Venus* was not so favoured, for it struck her Main Mast and splintered it together with her Main and Fore Top Masts and top Galland Masts, which was however soon remeded with others, and on the Evening of the 3d we made Bantom, and on the 4th we Anchored in Batavia Roads — being the 25th day from our departure from Bengal, and allowing the Five days spent at Kocatoir, was reckoned a very short passage.

At this point in the narrative, Frances left an empty space, in the centre of which she wrote, with a pale ink, very different from the darker ink of the rest of the journal:

> To be continued when I can find any
> data to go by, but a long train of
> misfortunes succeeded this part of
> the Voyage — of which I do not find
> any memorandum.

The passage between the Sooloo Islands presented the most beautiful scenery in the Known World. Nothing else-where could equal the Verdure, broad terraces of green sward in some places, and on the other parts of the Coast, Trees growing down to the Waters Edge; and generally a strong currant flowing between the Islands, which unfortunately were against us, and the weather being Calm, we could not make way against the streem all tho we made sail with every light Air that came off the Land. But altho they breathed the most luxurious perfume from these most fragrant islands, yet they were not strong enough to bear us on our Voyage, so that we were for three weeks buffeting with the Elements of Wind and Water, and when Night came, we found ourselves nearly in the spot from whence we started in the morning, altho we had been plying from shore to shore the whole day. And one evening in particular, we were greatly surprised by perceiving a sort of commotion in the water alongside, like a stream of water from a C and sure enough, the water was fresh, so that all hands were set to work, to fill up the casks; and altho the water was a little brackish, it served for a variety of purposes. Up to this time, the weather being fine, and by no means so hot as at Batavia, we consoled ourselves with fishing, and enjoying the various objects that serounded us, in these most beautiful straits — but alas a great misfortune was in store.

My beloved Husband was attacked with a dreadful disease, which is common to these Climats, a violent Colic but with the most extraordinary symptoms, and excruciating pain, attended with fever and distortions of every kind. Two Men could hardly restrain him, so as to prevent his hurting himself. He turned all colours, sometimes appearing as if Actually dead. After a time the symptoms abated, and he got over it, but it left him in a dreadfully debilitated state. But a similar disease deprived us of our dear little Patty, then a twelve Month old, saving one day. She died on board the *Halcyon* on the 15th day of April 1791 or 92.[9] A Leaden Box was prepared for her remains in order that they might be kept until we could Inter her remains in consicrated ground, in some Dutch settlement, and accordingly we made for the Island of Celebes. When after much negociation with the unfeeling Dutch Resident, and extortions of every kind, She was laid in a burying Ground situated opposite the place where we were at Anchor, from whence we watched the Ceremony, not being allowed to go on shore to pay the last duties to our dear Child. The spot where she is deposited is one of the most beautiful in the World — as are all the Spice Islands. There she lies under the Shade of a Grove of Cocoa Nut Trees.

Captain Barkley noted in his log dated April 5, 1792: "Interred my Dear Child in the burying ground ashore ..."

Death at sea was common and burials were attended to with care and ceremony. The bodies were typically placed in a canvas shroud which was loaded with ballast and then stitched closed. After the appropriate formalities the body was slipped over the side and flags flew at half-mast for a time in remembrance. The death of the master or a member of his family usually demanded more propriety. The body was placed in a coffin before being slid overboard or, in some cases, preserved in alcohol until it could be buried ashore at the earliest convenience. The Barkleys chose to bury their daughter at Celebes (now known as Sulawesi) which was the nearest port-of-call.

The island of Celebes is surrounded by a large and spectacular coral reef; a jewel for today's sports divers but the dread of early navigators. The shoreline is resplendent with coral white sand beaches which are offset by the deep blue of the sea. The island is mountainous, blanketed in noble palms and elegant tree ferns and framed by towering volcanic peaks. When Frances and Charles sailed into the bay on the south coast of Celebes, the scene that greeted them was one of a picturesque town with rows of villas and cottages, broad paths and pretty gardens. Past visitors said that it was the prettiest in the east. Frances herself remarked on the beauty of the area; perhaps that gave her some small comfort. Losing her baby was made worse by her being unable to accompany the tiny casket to the burial site. Harsh though it may seem, the Dutch guarded Celebes jealously and were very wary of the British trying to make inroads. The importance of Celebes for the Dutch was not so much in trade but more that the island was strategically situated as the geographical vanguard for control over the Dutch East Indies.

With fair winds the *Halcyon* and *Venus* turned out to sea that afternoon. Frances continues:

> After buffiting about from Island to Island, we made our passage between the Island of Gelolo and Margion into the Pacific Ocean. I never shall forget the beautiful scenery that these Islands presented to our View, as we sailed along their Coast, particularly on the two Islands which formed the narrow strait we pushed through at the rate of ten or twelve Knots an hour, impelled by a Rapid courant, and so narrow that we might have spoken to the persons on shore had there been any, and no depth could be found with ten fathom of line to the Lead. The Islands seemed like Fairy Land, rising in green Terraces one above another in the most graceful slopes, intersected with groves of Elegant Trees which seemed to fly past us as we rounded the projecting Points of Land, for Rocks or Clifts there were none, so that you seemed to be sailing on a beautiful River, between pleasure Grounds.
>
> to be continued
>
> In the Latitude _____ an the Longitude _____ we parted with the *Venus* our _____ As agreed upon, She to proceed to the Nt Wt

Coast of America, whilst we made the best of our Way to
Kamchatec persuant to the plan of the Expedition. The *Venus* was
a beautiful fast sailing Cutter. the Man whose Name was
Sheapard, was a great brute to his people and turned out a great
Rascal.

to be continued when I can find Data from the journal of the
Voyage

The note "to be continued … Voyage," is again written in a paler ink. At
this point Frances left a blank page to be filled in later. Then she continued:

On the 16th of June we had a glims of Land on the island of
Paramoucha, but so imperfect that we could not disern enough to
assertain where we were. It was so enveloped with fog.

Two and a half empty pages follow. It appears that after the death of
little Patty, Frances made no notes for some time, and was uncertain about
their track through the East Indies. Jilolo is an old name for the island of
Halmahera in the Northern Moluccas, and on the west side of Jilolo is a
small island spelled Macquian, probably Frances' Gelolo and Margion. Frances
then backtracked a month:

On the ____ day of May we fell in with one of the New Carolina Islands, which being laid down in the Spanish Maps very
erroneously, we made it very unexpectedly, at daylight, running at
the rate of ten knots an hour. We had a narrow escape, as we were
Sailing directly for it, so that our fate depended upon perhaps half
an hour longer dark, or had it been Foggy the Vessel would probably
have been lost, for the Shore was incompassed with sunken Rocks.
Some few Fishermen came off with a few Flying Fish which
they had no doubt for bait. They had not any fruit in the Canoe,
which was accounted for by their having been out on a fishing
expedition probably long before they discry'd our Vessel. However,
these Natives appear'd to have seen ships before, as they did not
show any sygns of Fear or astonishment. They would not Venture
on board for some time, but a few Spike Nails lowered down soon

The entry for April 23, 1792, in the logbook of the Halcyon.

Canoe with outriggers. Drawn by J. F. Whittingham.

brought them alongside, and they made fast their Fish, and a few triffling ornements which they wore in their Ears in exchange for Nails and some triffling presants. One Man only came on board out of forty or fifty who were along side in Nine Canoes. The Men were a large well proportioned People with fine regular features with very Bushy Hair hanging loose on their shoulders. They wore Caps made of a sort of neat matting in the shape of a sugar loaf, and they had Tortois shell Bracelets on their arms, and a kind of coarse Cornelian strung for necklaces, as well as Correll. Their Ears were perforated, to which were appended large Shells which had elongated the apurtures. They were very much Tatooed, and stained in differand paturns all over their Bodies. They looked clean and healthy, very differant from the Malays. They seemed to understand a few words that were spoken to them in the Language of the Sandwich Island, which people they resemble in their gestures, and Manner, but they are of a much lighter colour, and not quite so athletic.

Their Canoes were very large, made of planks sew'd together, rather high out of the Water but very narrow, and sharp at each end. In the Middle they have a platform of planks raised about two feet above the sides of the Canoes and it extends beyond the sides to which they have an out Rigger and a log of Wood to the Weather side, fastened to act as a balance. They sett on this platform, and take shelter under it probably by Night, but when under sail all the spare hands get on the weather outrigger to keep the Canoe from oversetting. They have a very tall Mast and a large sail made of Matting, and Sail very fast, and when they alter their course they Shift the Sails without turning the Canoe, which being both ends alike, no matter which end is foremost. They are very clean and painted in stripes Red and White. Upon standing inn for the Shore we saw an emense Number of Canoes, or Prows, for they were very large, but they brought us but little fruit, a few Cocoa Nuts and some trash for which they were anxious to get Iron.

The Island to wich they gave the name of Yapp, looked very beautifully wooded, and their Houses, which we saw very distinctly with a telescope (being not more than a mile from the shore) were well built, the best we had seen in the South Sea, and looked like our Farm Houses, with slaunting Roofs, and altogether a large Village. In fact we were surprised at their poverty, for in other respects they answer the discription given by Capten Wilson of the Pelew Islands, and the Natives seemed to understand the words given in his vocabulary of the language of those Islands. In fact, if the pronounciation had been correct, we should have found the same here, and they talk very fast and loud.

We had a very smart breeze as we stood along the island, and the Prows kept up wonderfully with our Vissel, which being coppered bottomed sailed very well. We stood out to sea in the afternoon, but the wind falling in the Evening it became calm, and to our surprise we saw two canoes make their appearance, and soon after several others, altho we were from three to four leagues from the Shore. They came from the West end of the Island, where we saw a large well peopled Village situated in a grove of Cocoa nutts. It looked very green and pleasant to the Eye, altho there was no appearance of cultivation. We were very glad that the Night proved Calm, for the poor sailors, for when we stood off it had a very differant appearance.

to be continued.

The six empty pages which follow represent five or six weeks of time. The numbers "91 or 92" in the entry following are written in pale ink, undoubtedly added at a later time.

> On the 16th of June 91 or 92
> Made South Island, So called by Captn. Gore, who was the first who visited it, and discovered it. We were the Next Vessel that made the dangerous Rock for it hardly deserves the Name of an Island. It looks like a large high bluff Rock rising from the Sea, the Surge breaking violently on its rugged front. There being no beach, being thus perpendicular, it was not possible to Land on. Captn Barkley rowed up to it, and survey'd it in all directions, but in vain. Its Top was lost in thick Clouds so that we could not see its height, but from the convulsed agetation of the Clouds, it was agreed by all hands that it must be a Volcana. There was no other way of accounting for the strange appearance it exhibited, as there was a constant rising of the Clouds as if occasioned by some Explosion altho we could not actually see any colom of smoke or fire arise. There were a few Boobys perched here and there, but no doubt destitute of any human Inhabitants. The existence of this Island has been much doubted, therefore our falling in with it gave great satisfaction to Nautical Men.
> to be continued.

Both this entry and the one which follows are dated June 16. Two and a half blank pages separate the South Island paragraph from the incomplete sentence about Sulphur Island.

> Altho we passed very near Sulphur Island we did not see it, altho Captn. Barkley was very desirous of making it &

Sulphur Island is now commonly known as Iwo Jima. It is not surprising that the Barkleys missed seeing it; although dominated by the 190-metre Mount Suribachi volcano of World War Two fame, the island is small, only

20 square kilometres. Iwo Jima has always been famed for its sulphur beds which is perhaps why the Barkleys wanted to visit.

KURILE ISLANDS AND KAMCHATKA PENINSULA

Once they left the traffic of the Southeast Asian trade routes, Captain Barkley needed to pay particular attention to his navigational instruments. At the time the *Halcyon* was making its way into these northern latitudes the coastlines had not been charted in any systematic way nor were there established sailing routes to follow. Caution and alertness were critical for a successful passage. As they moved farther north into the shroud of thick fog banks and cloud-covered skies, navigation became difficult. A clear sky is needed to observe the positions of the sun, moon, planets and stars, and thus fix the position of the ship. Without daily calculations it was easy to become lost.

On the 16th of June we had a Glimpse of Land appearing like a Mountain of Snow but it soon vanished and the former dull scene was renewed, nothing but fog and Mist. Indeed the whole of this forlorn locality is most dreary. The transition was very trying, from the beautiful bright sky we left behind us. Having so recently too injoy'd fine summer weather, the change was greatly felt by the poor Lascars, who never felt cold before. It made me very Ill too, and caused my face to swell and my teeth to ache. This was the first Illness I experienced from being on board Ship ... having from the very first of my Voyages been blessed with good health, which gave me courage to endure danger, and to submit to privation.

On the 17th we again made the Land, which proved to be the South End of the Island of Paramocha, the Northernmost of the Kurile Islands, seperated from the Main Land by a Narrow Strait, the weather still miserably Cold and comfortless with a drizzling Rain and thick Fog and mist, which made our situation not only disagreeable but dangerous.

In the afternoon the dull uniformity of the scene was cheered by announcement from the Mast Head of a Sail in view, in fact a Russian Galliot, which was standing across us, and would probably have escaped our notice If the Fog had not cleared away a little. Great must have been their astonishment at being Hailed by a foreign Vessel in those Seas. As soon as they Spyed the Colours they altered their course and ran before the Wind, but the *Halcyon* being coppered, we soon came up with them. She was last from Ste. Peter & St. Paul two days from thence, bound to Ochotck where she belonged. She bore the appearance of antiquity in her build, very bulky and misshapen, and without any orniment whatever, the bare planks shewing without Paint or even Tar, her Sails if possible more awkward than her Hull, as well as her Rigging which displayed less ingenuity even than any thing we ever saw. She had been on a cruze amongst the Islands and came direct from Awatcha Bay.

Captn. B. went on board her but found great difficulty in making himself understood. However, he confermed our situation on the Chart which corresponded with his own reckoning, for he had not been able to take an observation, not even for the Latitude, for several days. He likewise bought some sables which they produced at sight of a Cask of English Porter with which he had provided himself, as well as some Madeira Wine, which was very acceptable to an Invalid who was on board, who had nothing to offer in return. But his lady, a very handsome Young Woman who was with him, sent me a pritty small Sable Muff and wished very much to come on board our Vessel to see an English Woman, as did several of the Passengers, particularly the Women, of whom there were several on board; but their Captain, who appeared as uncouth as the Bark he commanded, would not allow. However, he came on board himself, and brought a few skins, for which he extorted double their value in necessaries of which they were destitute. However, the Ladies all stood upon Deck and we nodded and laughed and I was delighted to see anything in the shape of rational beings. I believe they were European Women — very fair and good looking. There is a constant intercourse between the Islands and the Main, and at Ochotch there are many Russians sittled.

Captn. B. was likewise so fortunate as to procure from the Sailors several Dogskin Great Coats which proved a very seasonable supply to the poor Lascars, who were perishing with Cold. Indeed

Avacha Bay.

the wet & Foggs we met with was even worse than the gales of wind and cold we had encountered during our passage. At this time the Sea was very high but it was nearly Calm, so that we were glad to get clear of the Galliot. The Sailors who accompanied the Captain on Board, looked like English Sailors, and the Passengers were very fine looking Men, whose Dress under their Skin Coats consisted of Smock Frocks, gaged as our Farmers Men wear theirs, very neatly made and clean and smart. They were traders, no doubt. The men to the number of ten and twelve came on board, and were regaled with Rum and water, but they remained perfectly sober and appeared very gentle and well behaved — the Russian Language in which they conversed is a very soft Language, More like Italian than any of the Northern dialects.

On the 19th June we had a transient view of the Coast of Kamchatca, to the South Cape Gavaria — the Land made in high Hills covered with Snow, and altho we did not expect to see such a wintery scene, yet it was Land, and as such pleasant to the Eye. But it soon vanished again in the thick Fog, which must have hid the Land whilst we were coasting the Shore, no very pleasant reflection on such an unfrequented Coast as this Pinunsula.

On the 20th, the weather having cleared, we again saw Land to the North of that seen the preceeding day, which presented a still more Magnificent appearance. At the same time it bore the most dreary Aspect, high mountains Clad with Snow from the

Summit to the very Waters Edge, the Tops however hid by a thick mist, which continued to hover over the Peaks, adding thereby to their apparent height. We were in great hopes of reaching the Bay of Awatcha, so as to get into Port before night, but about Noon the Breeze died away and left us all together in the Evening, only a few leagues from the destined Port. However, to our great relief a small Breeze soon after sprung up, and allowed us to get an offing. Captn. Barkley being alarmed at being so near an unfrequented shore, in a dead Calm. And the next morning proved very fine, so that in the afternoon the setting sun shone in great splendour and made the Snow so bright that it almost put our Eyes out, appearing like Mountains of polished Silver rising from the bosom of the Ocean. We tryed our fishing lines in the hope of catching Cod Fish (which are said to be very abundant) but without success.

On the 21st we saw the long saught Light house situated on the point of Land which formes the entrance of Awatcka Bay, and our old Enemy the Fog having taken its departure, and the three Mountains, with the Volcana smoking, made a sublime object. The alteration of weather when we became Imbay'd was surprising. We seemed to have passed from Winter to Summer in a few hours. Still however, the snow did not melt at four oclock in the afternoon. We werc abreast of the lighthouse and at six being

Town of St. Peter and St. Paul (Petropavlovsk). Drawn by J.F. Whittingham.

pretty near the Town of St. Peter and St. Paul, we were surprised
by the report of three great Guns, and soon perceived the smoke
to proceed from a point of narrow Land very conveniantly situated
for the protection of the Town. A Boat was immediately dispatched. They met a canoe comming off with a Pilot to indicate
the place where the Vessel was ordered to cast Anchor. The spit of
Land before mentioned is guarded by a Sargeant and a few
Soulders, who were drawn up, with their Muskets Shouldered, but
they looked more like Bears than Men, being clad in the Skins of
that Animal. The Village makes but a miserable appearance, the
view of it taken by Mr. Webber is very correct, and there does not
appear any alterations since Captain King visited this settlement.
The Harbour is Magnificent. The Hills run sloping down to the
water's edge leaving only space for the Village, which, however,
contains more Inhabitants than at first Sight would be imagined,
the Winter habitations being all under ground so that all that
appears of them is a Mount of earth.

When the Barkleys entered Petropavlovsk on the Kamchatka Peninsula to
trade in pelts, the Russian fur trade was well established. Petropavlovsk was the
centre of trade on the coast but it was carefully guarded. The Russians had the
peltry to themselves and were not favourably disposed to open trade to outside
competition, particularly to British vessels. Just 13 years earlier in 1778, when
Captain Cook was surveying the Alaska coast, he was warned by a Russian
trader and administrator that without a letter of introduction from him for
safe passage into the Port of Avacha Bay, he would surely be shot at with a
cannon. It was not until the Tsarist government concluded treaty agreements
with Britain and the United States in 1824 and 1825 that trade was openly
welcomed. However, the fur traders brought with them many products of
civilization that were in short supply in these outpost communities, so clan-
destine trading often took place on the sly and under the pretext of ceremony
and hospitality. It was a time-consuming and expensive process.

The Vessel is Moored in a lac or Basin which is nearly inclosed
on all sides, and the water as smooth as a Lake & so transparent
that the Shadows of the serounding objects, particularly of the

Governer of the place, as we pass'd the
low spit the gard was draw up and
like wise at the grand gaurd ...
and as soon as we came in sight of
the major's house two "ladys came down
to meet us. who prov'd the Capt. & sargt
wifes they conducted me up to the —
house at the door of which the major
met us and conducted us after a few com
plements not a word of which I understod
in to the house, which is clean and comfor
table, much like a little cottage in Engla
nd, the chairs and table of deal as white
as snow, the women were the most unac
countable figures of the whole old & ugly
but what is better than beauty they seem to posses

This page is probably from Frances Barkley's missing Diary.

114

Volcanoe in the distance, has a very imposing Effect, and the Village in the foreground is very Picturesque and our own Vessel and the Boats rowing about the little Harbour enlivened and Peopled the scene.

The Kamchadale Village on the spit of Land makes a very shabby appearance. A leutenant resides at it with a Sargents Guard, but the Governor, who is a Major in the Army, resides on the opposite side of the Harbour, on the slope of a Hill. His house or Isba as they call the kind of House he lives in, resembles a neat English farm house of a middling Class, or more in the style of a Welsh Cottage. There is a small Garden in the front, and a little to the right a small Landing place, on which are mounted Six Guns, and on a platform above, the Main Guard are drawn up, consisting of a few Kamchatca souldiers, and a few stand of Arms are piled not unlike one of our very smallest Coast Guard Stations, not, however, in the grotesque figures that Man it. So that with the guns on the Spit of Land on the other side, they seem to have more guns than Men.

As soon as we came to an Anchor the Sergeant came on board with Compliments from the Governer, and a present of two large Salmon, which the Sergeant assured us had been buried several days to fit it for the Governers table, no recommendation to us altho with wry faces we were obliged to swallow it. He likewise brought us an invitation to dine the next day with the Governor, Major Ismailov, and accordingly the next day at Noon the second in Command, Captn. Rosterguff, came to escort us on Shore. As we passed the Spit of Land, the Guard was drawn up to salute us, and when we came to the Main Guard we received the like compliment. As soon as we landed I was met by two Ladies who proved to be the Captn and the Sergeants Wives. They conducted me with much ceremony up to the house, where the Major stood in full Uniform to Meet us at the door. After a compliment not a word of which we understood, he gave Me his Arm and led us into his House, which is neat and clean and really very comfortable, furnished with deal Tables and Chairs as white as Snow, and the Women altho old and very Ugly were very friendly and polite. The Governor appeared rather out of Place amongst them, being quite a Gentleman in manner. He appolagized by gistures, for the homely repast we had to expect, which consisted of one of the same sort of prepared Salmon, and by way of giving me a prefferance, I was helped to the Snout of the fish, which was reckoned a great luxery. It was quite putrid & I was obliged to acknolidge myself a snob by prefering a slice of the fresh Fish which was served at the bottom of the table for inferior guests.

The rest of the dinner consisted of Cranberries, Salt Fish, and what they call bread altho it is made of Salmon Row, reduced to a powder and then seasoned and a few shreds of the Salmon mixed with it, the whole kneeded together and fermented with something like Yeast, and then Baked in a Tin. It cuts like bread and is no bad substitute. The repast was not a little prized by the introduction of a fine Chechire Cheese and some bottled Porter which unexpectedly made its appearance, which was much relished. After that we had Cranbery puffs (what the paste was made of I know not) and Punch with Cranburies instead of Lemon juice.

After dinner we took a strole to the Landing place, and were gratified to find the snow was beginning to Melt, and wild flowers begin to peep out. In due time Tea was served of the finest flavour, and sweetened with very fine Sugar Candy. These articles they get over Land from China, and they likewise produced some hard bisquits. Soon after tea we got into our Boat well pleased to get rid of the civilities of the company, and we had a delightful Row round the Bay of Awatchca, in order to see if we could detect any spot on which we could promise ourselves a Walk. We found the Snow disappearing in patches, but no appearance of a footpath.

Major Ismailow is an Elderly Man, rather corpulant. He spoke a few words of English. He promised us a Visit on board the Next day, and gave us to understand that he had sent for a Cow and some Beef & Poultry in order to entertain us better on our next Visit, likewise some Vegetables. He has a Farm about five miles inland, where he resides in general, only Visiting St. Peter & St. Paul occasionally, he being Governor of the Provence.

The next day they all came on board, and in addition a fine little Boy of his, about five years old, and a smart Young Kamschatca Woman, all drest in their best, and looked a decent party, the Kamschadale woman very fine indeed. She was dressed in the fashion of the Country, with a full Bodied Chemise Dress, with large full sleeves of very fine Linin, fastened with a gold botton at the Coller and pleated very fine like a habit shirt; over it a vest tight to the waist, fastened down with sugar loaf Bottons, with a very full short Cloth Petticoat, coloured Stockings and Low topped Shoes & silver Buckles. She is a handsome woman, fair skin rather en bonpoint, very shy, and seemed out of her Place, but as the other Women patronised her, and the little Boy seemed very fond of her, we did not think it necessary to enquire much about her. The Major gave us to understand she was in attendance on his Child. She sat down to table as a matter of course and soon got very merry.

The Major presented me on coming on board with 10 fine Red Fox Skins called Shevadowsky's. They are marked on the Back with a White Cross, and he gave Captn Barkley a very handsome sea otter skin. His little Boy also came prepared with a presant of two sable skins, which he gave to our little William, who was delighted to get a playfellow, altho he proved a rough one.

We gave them an excellent dinner, poultry, pork, fish and soup, besides pastry and preserves which we had in abundance from Calcutta and Batavia, besides what they liked better — plenty of Wine, Beer, brandy and Rum. They were all very jolly, and the day passed off very pleasantly. They all seemed to like our good Cheer, particularly the Liquids. They have no Liquors excep a kind of stuff they call Quass. I fancy it is what we call Mead. But I fear Captn B. made too great a display of Generosity, for they all took a fancy to something or other, and none went away empty handed.

Captn B. hoped therby to conceliate the Governer, so as to enable him to trade freely with the Kamschatcadales, but he soon found that they were only permitted to trade by stealth. They used to come with their skin Bag stuffed with Sables after dark, and at first a brisk trade was carried on, but as nothing was to be done without Brandy and Rum, they soon misbehaved, and Betray'd themselves, and it was soon seen that their Numbers fell off. Captn B. remonsterated with the Governer but he made more & more professions of Friendship & got more and more presents to very little purpose. The Russians seem a treacherous set.

The next day we went on Shore to visit the Hamlet, and called on the Captn's Wife. She shew'd us her House, which was very neat and clean. Her Bed Chamber was very neat and clean. All the Rooms are on the ground floor, and the houses generally consist of four Rooms with a stove in the Middle opening like an oven in the Kitchin, and in the opening everything is Cooked. I fancy there are seperate stoves contrived at the side, for the Main opening seemed to be full of fuel night & day and throue out a great heat, and the three other appartments are so contrived as to abut on the stove and are all warmed by it, something like a German Stove. The three appartments consist of a sitting Room & two BedRooms. This formes an Isba, of which there are about 9 in the Village of St. Peter & St. Paul, about an equal number of Yourts which are underground. There are about three of four Balangans or Summer habitations.

The Village on the Spit of Land, which I believe is more properly styled the Town, consists of about thirty Balangans, no Yourts but about 10 Isbas, the inhabitants all very civilised and the Children even courtious, the girls really very pretty. They run out of their huts and before you are aware of it Kiss your hands and even the hem of your Garments, the better Sort expecting to be allowed to kiss your forehead; I mean the women, for the Men seem as stupid as the Women were Cheer-ful and polite. All are for dragging you into their houses, and all have some thing to offer — mostly Cranburries, which are very large, fine and well flavoured. We were gratified to see the snow all melted, and a track like a sheep Walk becoming visible. We ascended a little way, followed by all the Children in the Village, all of whom wanted to Caress little William, who was glad enough to frolick and play with them; and we had many pleasant walks after that, always taking care to land at a distance from the regular landing place. We preferred scrambling up the Rocks to the annoyance of being followed.

It would have been a welcome break for William to play with children his own age. With only adults around to observe, he probably acted and sounded like a mini adult. Many a young child raised aboard had only the crew for role models and it was not uncommon to hear shipboard children swear a blue streak, despite the protestations of their parents.

By this time, the 24th of June, the snow had entirely disappeared, and strange to say the Banks that arose behind the Rocks were covered with Wild Flower, Shrubs and Roots. There were several sorts of Ever Greens begun to shake off their Winter Coats, so that the Country really looked green and pretty, but very difficult of access — however the south sides of the Hills are well wooded. Every day presented fresh beauties in the vegetable world. Never did I witness such quick vegetation. The south banks were covered with a profusion of wild Flowers in the short space of Time that we remained, and the heat was intolerable, and swarms of Flys infested us, so that our evening walks were rendered disagreeable by them, particularly if we happened to stray from the Main Path, which

Avacha Bay.

soon became trodden by the Kamchadates, who went backwards & forwards to Verchenea where Major Ismalow seemed to keep all his stores. We soon had a variety of preserved fruits, principally different sorts of which they enumerated: Strawberries, bil Berries, hurtle berries, wortle berries and Black Berries, all of which they preserve a great quantity. We likewise partook of a sort of bread made of a Root resembling a Lilly Root, which was really pleasant to the taste. The Major likewise sent us some new laid Eggs, and Milk every morning, our goats not yeilding a very good supply.

About a Week after our arrival, we had a Visit from the Padra Papa, whose title Corresponds with our Bishops. He was attended by the Priest of Paratoinska where there is a church. We hear he had likewise his Wife with him. They appeared very sociable, partook of our good Cheer. The Papa looked more like a jew Rabba than anything else. There were likewise some good looking Men with him, Merchants. They wore Silk Shirts, and a sort of Dowlas frock, made very neatly. They all became very merry before we parted, which was not until the Next day. They slept on the Cabin Floor, such as could not be accommodated with Beds.

The next day we dined on shore with the Major, whose table presented a very differant appearance to what it did on our first Visit. It was now spread with a damask Table Cloth instead of a coarse brown cloth, blue earthen ware instead of wooden platters, & pewter dishes and glass instead of horns, all of which articles Captn B. presented him with, as well as Wine & Beer, Cheese &&c. I likewise presented Mrs. Rosterguff with a Tea set of real china, in return for which she gave me two sables, and the Bed quilt from her Bed, which was made of Silk & lined with Squirrel skins, with a border of sea otter skins. She likewise gave me a very warm Pelise or Cloak, for it partook of the Character of both, and altho pritty well worn, was very acceptable of an Evening; for altho the sun shone intensily hot, yet there was always a Chill from the snow that still covered the Mountains of an evening. Nothing material occured in this visit. The Major gave us an excellent dinner. There was no end to the dishes, which were served one by one, and very good pastry. Indeed all their food seemed well cooked, and flavoured. We had something like a syllabub[10] after dinner, and prodigiously fine Fish, principally salmon dressed in all Manner of ways.

I rather think the Major does not reside much at Petropavlowsky but occasionally, and that the Isba is the residance of Captn Rosterguff, who commands the Station, and that the Major who is the Governer of the Provence resides in Bolscheretsk in the Winter and Verchenea in the Summer. How it happened that he was here so early in the year I know not, unless to get supplys from the Galliot before mentioned from Okotck. The Garrison seemed very badly off, but as they consist principally of Kamchadales, their wants are soon supplied, and the few Cossacks that are kept here live in the same manner, and are all married to Kamchadale women. They are, however, fine looking Men and carry Arms, which the Kamchadales are not allowed. Major Ismalow seemed to be liked. He succeeded Major Bymn in the command of the province. *He,* however, seems to have been a very differant Character, as narated in Captn King's narative. Nothing matirial occurred. Captn B. got a few Skins by driblets, and the Governer kept up appearances by sending us a supply of vegetables from his Farm at Verchney, which seemes about a days journey from hence.

The Petro Papa left the Bay on the 20th in his ____ on his way to the Kurile Islands, which he visits once in three years. I do not know the object of this Visitation, but I suppose to conferm the Inhabitants of these Islands, who all profess the Greek religion.

Although the Russian Orthodox Church did not establish its first mission in Alaska until 1794 there were earlier frontier missionaries who brought the Russian Orthodoxy of the Tsarina Catherine the Great to outpost communities. These missionaries were often very poor, selling candles and books and sacrificing their own salaries to meet the needs of their parishes, such was their passion. The Petro Papa was most likely going to tend to his ministry among the Aleuts.

There is not a hut in St. Peter & St. Paul that has not a saint hung up in a rude Frame, and they say their prayrs before it as they do in the Romish church. It was unfortunate for us, we think, that the Governor was on the Station, for it was his duty to prevent the Kamchadales disposing of their Furs, with which they pay their tribute to the Empress. The Captn and his Wife, we think, would have winked at the Trade. It would have been easier at any rate to conciliate them, than to have to bribe a Man in a higher station. Not that the Government got one Skin the more for our loss for the Kamchadales hide their Furs until they have an opportunity of bartering them away for Brandy and other necessaries with the periodical Merchants, who come from Ochotsk.

On the 27th of the Month, the whole Ostrog was alarmed by the intelligance of a Vessel in sight from the Light House. She soon after Anchored in the Outer Bay and proves to be a Russian Frigate last from Ocotck. We found that she formed a part of an Expedition sent from Russia on a Voyage of discovery, commanded by Captn Billings, who, however, did not come with the Frigate, having been Landed at Ischutshoisnoss with the intintion of exploring Bearings Straits by the Land, for which he is provided with Canoes & natives of the differant Tribes of Asiatics who inhabit this part of Siberia, who do not acknowlidge the Alegiance of Russia. Therefore it is considered a very hazardous undertaking, but Billings is represented as a very enterprising Character. The Frigate which appeared to be about eight hundred Tons Burden, was Commanded by the second Captn, who is an English Man (Captn Hall), brought up in the Russian Service, rather a low bred Man, with great pretensions. We saluted the Frigate with seven Guns, which was returned with five. However, Captn Hall came on board, was mighty Civel, and in his turn took a fancy to whatever he saw; and on the second day after her arrival, being the Annaversary of the Empress's Birth Day, we dined on board, together with the Governer.

We were received with much ceremony. The Ship was decorated with evergreens, the yards were Man'd, and a band of music play'd, I suppose, patriotic Airs. The Frigate was well Man'd and Officered and she was very clean and everything in order. Captn Hall gave us a good dinner, and as soon as the cloth was removed, the Empress's health was given a salute of 21 guns, then the Arch Duke and Dutchess with 19 guns, the rest of the Royal Family with 19 guns, the King of England with an equal number, Captn Barkley and Mrs. Barkleys health and success to the *Halcyon* with 15 guns, the Governor of Kamchatca and the Garison with 15 guns. We passed the afternoon with great harmony, and about three in the afternoon a Cutter belonging to the Expidition came into the Bay and saluted the Fort with seven guns. Likewise, the Frigate, which was returned with 5. The *Halcyon* likewise saluted her with 7 guns, which she returned with 5.

After these ceremonies the Captain of her came on board the Frigate, and was introduced in form. Both Officers and Men were in their Uniforms. The Officers of the Navy when in full dress wear nearly the same Uniform as the Army, but Captn Hall wore the same as the Major, green turned up with white and two Epauletts, altho only a Captn. The Gentleman who commanded the Cutter is a very gentell Man, and all the Officers of both Ships were very Cevil and attentive, altho very reserved with respect to the plans of the Expedition.

We however learned that it consisted of two Frigates besides store ships and a Frigate in frame, which with all sorts of Artisans & tools were convey'd overland to Yakutsk on the River Lena, which was to be the rendevous of the differant branches of the Expidition. The Frigates sailed from Archangle with a View of surveying the River Covimar or Kovimar, with the hope of finding a Pasage into the North Pacific Ocean, or if possible to double Shagotskoy Noss, and round to Bearings Straits so as to compleat the discovery of that passage round East Cape, but they lost one Frigate at the Mouth of the River Kovima, and were a long time building the Frigate they brought in Frame. Whether it was intended to Navigate the Lena down to the Sea or not, we could not make out, but they explored the River Kovima and brought away Petrifactions of branches of Trees which must have been buried for Centuries. Captn Hall gave me some valuable specimens. Had they not lost the Frigate at the Mouth of this River, they expected to have made their way from it into the Anadur, for there it was that the Frigate now here was

Stationed, and it was from thence that Captn Billings was set a going as the high Land of which Ischutshois-Noss

The Frigate and Cutter we have now in the Sound must have met the Expedition, from Europe

This section of the *Reminiscences* ends abruptly and is followed by a blank space of a page and a half.

Frances does not mention the name of Martin Sauer, secretary to the expedition, who was probably present at the thundering celebration of the birthday of the Empress. Sauer was the author of *An account of a geographical & astronomical expedition to the northern parts of Russia,* published in 1802, "performed by command of Her Imperial Majesty Catherine the Second, by Commodore Joseph Billings, in the years 1785–1794." It is interesting to view the Barkleys through Martin Sauer's eyes:

On the 16th, after encountering a few contrary gales and baffling calms, we arrived in the bay of Avatcha, in a very thick fog (which fell upon us at the mouth of the bay), and came to anchor near the entrance into the inner harbour of St. Peter and St. Paul, without being able to see any land.

Notwithstanding we were as silent as possible on board, with a view of surprising the inhabitants when the weather became a little clear, we had not lain long before we heard a boat rowing towards the vessel; and were shortly after amazed at seeing an English pinnace coming alongside, with Captain Charles William Barkley in it, whose vessel, the *Alcyon,* from Bengal, was at anchor in the inner harbour on a trading voyage. His cargo consisted of articles that were invaluable in this part of the world; particularly in a port so eligibly situated for encouraging commercial undertakings; namely, iron in bars, anchors, cables, and cordage, with various kinds of ironmongery wares, and a considerable stock of rum.

Notwithstanding this, the commander of the port having neither authority nor resolution to secure a purchase for account of government; and the traders of this peninsula (who stile themselves merchants) being merely a set of roving pedlars, without either capital or credit (and, what is still worse, without principles to secure either); Captain Barkley was necessitated to take these articles back again, although they were offered at less than one third of the charges of transporting such commodities from the manufactories in Siberia.

A man who has resolution to strike out a new line of commerce, or rather to seek a new source of trade, in parts of the world so little known as are these regions, at the same time unacquainted with the language and with the wants of the inhabitants, is rather threatened with loss, than flattered with prospects of profit, in the first attempt; and nothing short of enthusiastic hope of future advantages can compensate for the degree of anxiety that he must suffer. Such a man, most certainly, merits all the encouragement that the government can give him, which is sure to be eventually benefited by his success. Considering these circumstances, and that the two vessels employed in our expedition were in the greatest need of entire new rigging, anchors, &c. the present favourable opportunity of serving Captain Barkley by clearing his ship was a secondary consideration, compared to the advantages which government would have derived from so valuable an acquisition of the most necessary articles that the port could possess. This I represented to the governor of the port, and to the commanding officers of our expedition; but both equally feared to act without positive orders. In other respects, however, we gave him all the assistance in our power.

Captain Barkley was accompanied by his lady, and a son of about seven years old. Their behaviour was very polite, and particularly pleasing to us. I lament that we were not able to make them equal returns, but flatter myself that they were satisfied with our endeavours. The extreme poverty of the place, and the miserable situation that we were in, must have been sufficient in their eyes to prove an excuse for us. They left this place the 1st July O.S."[11]

Sauer added, in a footnote, that a second frigate, the *Black Eagle*, commanded by Captain Saretcheff, arrived on the 19th.

Frances' view of the "assistance" of the Russian naval frigates differs considerably from Sauer's:

> To return to our own persuits, I have only to add that as it was
> proposed on board the Frigate to renew the Convivialities of the
> Feast, in order to entertain Captn. Serichief, the Captn of the
> Cutter, we took our departure, as did many of the party, after
> being regaled with Tea, of which they use the finest quality in this
> far distant Land, which with sugar Candy to sweeten it are
> brought over Land from China.
>
> Upon our leaving the Frigate we were again saluted with a
> broadside and also with three Cheers. The Governor brought us on
> shore, but we were glad to part company on the Landing, glad to
> escape from any more ceremonious cevility, and indeed a little quiet
> was very acceptable after the Noise and bustle of the day. We took a
> walk round a part of the craggy sides of the Cliffs that over looked
> the Bay, and were delighted with the appearance of it, enlivened by
> the Ships of War, and our own little Brig all decked with the Flags
> of all nations, our own little Union flying at our Mast Head as well
> as from every other conspicuous place, besides being displayed on
> the Flag Staff. We contemplated it with actual devotion, delighted as
> we felt at the knolidge that we were the free subjects of the happy
> Country whose banner we owned, for notwithstanding appearances,
> we saw enough on board the Russian to bless God that we were not
> under its Sway.
>
> The Boats, two skimming from side to side, made the scene
> very cheerful. Captn. B. having made a Signal for his Boat, we
> embarked, and were saluted by Cheers when we passed under the
> stern of the Frigate, the Company on board being very noisy; but
> every thing on the Land was serene and quiet, and a clear bright
> Moon prolonged the elusion which seemed to transport us to our
> own dear Country.
>
> After this we were constantly visited, morning, Noon & night,
> by these Strangers, who ate us out of house & home. The effects of
> the profusion of hospitality expended on them we had reason to
> lament in more ways than one afterwards, for they acted as Spies

under the Mask of Friendship, and we soon found that the Kamchatcadales were more and more timid, and never brought their Furs to barter except by stealth. Captn Barkley complained to the Governer, who confessed that they were ordered to refrain from their Visits, on acct of the effects of the Spirits for which they sold their Skins, this when the whole party were drinking Wine without limit at our expense. Besides every one of the people having secured a portion of Rum for his own use, was too bad. And then these New Comers extorted from the Kamchadales every Skin they could detect, under pretence of Collecting the Empress's tribute. The Governer was rather the best of the Party, but he seemed in great awe of the Navy Men, and soon left the Ostrog to go to Vercheney, from whence he sent a Cow and Calf and Vegetables of different Sorts as a sort of farewell present.

And the day following we saw the Cutter get under Weigh, and we found she was sent to Ownalaska, evidently in order to Collect the Furs there, so as to be before hand with us. From all this it was but too clear that nothing was to be done in the way of Trade. All this time Captn Hall was constantly proposing some kind of amusement to lull our suspicions, and on one occasion he had a

Abruptly the Kamchatkan section of the *Reminiscences* ends. Frances left three and a half blank pages, which were never filled in. From a section of the log of the *Halcyon* it is known that the vessel left Avacha Bay on July 20, 1792, sailing eastward; 27 days later the company of the ship saw the white cone of Mount St. Elias, in Alaska.

The Northwest Coast.

Chapter Seven
Alaska, Hawaii and Cochin China

ALASKA

*T*owering above the clouds that ring its crest, the sharp, icy peak of Mount St. Elias represents the largest mountain range in North America. It has stood as an imposing beacon for seafarers since the earliest vessel broached these waters. Captain Vitus Bering, commander of the *St. Peter*, first saw Mount St. Elias on July 16, 1741, while on an expedition mapping the coast and he may have named the spectacular peak. Thirty-seven years later, Cook sighted and named Mount Edgecumbe without landing, before sailing directly to Prince William Sound. In the following years there were arrivals from others nations: La Pérouse, Dixon, Malaspina and others. It was upon this view that Frances looked out from the deck of the *Halcyon*. In her *Reminiscences* she wrote:

> On the 16th of August, 1792, we made the Coast of America again, in two places, the Northern and Southern extremes of Beerings Bay, with Mount St. Elias & Mount Fairweather in view. They are both very high mountains, with their Heads covered with Snow. The weather at this time was tolerabley warm, but misty and like the weather we met with on the Coasts of Asia, very changeable & at times chilly. The wind being Unfavourable, and the Coast entirely unknown, we did not reach a port of safity

until the 18th, and then farther to the North than Captn Barkley originally intended. The Land formed a Deep Bay, Called Admiralty Bay, a sound of great extent with many Harbours in it. The one in the which we cast Anchor is called Lord Mulgrave's Harbour. The Country looked Green and pleasant to the Eye, the Anchorage safe and snug.

The *Halcyon* was now in the ancestral waters of the Tlingit, the northernmost group of the northwest coast peoples. Tucked among the inlets of the coastal mountains they created wealthy societies founded upon the abundant resources of the sea and the forests. Highly skilled navigators and astute traders, they never assumed that Europeans were superior. They made slaves of their captives and were widely feared, and explorers and traders had met their fate at the hands of the Tlingit on more than one occasion. Captain Alexi Chirikov, sailing as consort to Bering in the *St. Paul,* suffered the loss of some of his crew in Tlingit territory. Beset by weather Chirikov became separated from Bering but was able eventually to reach Sitka Sound. Desperate for supplies he sent a small boat ashore with ten men; when it failed to return he sent a search party of five. They also disappeared, all apparently at the hands of the Tlingit.

Frances was the first European woman to visit the Alaskan coast. She reported the Tlingit to be "the most dangerous and mischevious set we had ever Met." Of their meeting she writes:

> Several canoes soon hove in sight, some from Fishing and some with women on board. They appeared most disgusting objects, covered with greasy Sea otter Skins, with the Fur to the Skin and the

A chief of Port Mulgrave. Drawn by a Spanish artist.

leather Tanned Red, and beyond description dirty. It was here we first saw women with those pieces of shaped wooden Lip ornaments which are discribed in Cap. Cooks Voyages — if such a frightful apendage can be called ornimental, a thing that distorts the Mouth, and gives the whole Features a new and most unpleasant Character. The piece of wood is inserted into a slit made in the under Lip when the females are about fourteen years old, and it is replaced from Year to Year, larger and larger, until in Middle Age it is as large as the bowl of a table spoon; and it is nearly the same shape to appearance, being concave on the inside of the Lip, which it presses out from the Gum, thereby shewing the whole of the teeth and Guins, a frightful sight at best, but of Still worse when the Teeth are black and dirty which theirs were invariably, generally uneven & decayd; and this odious Mouth piece so compleatly disfigured them that it was impossible to tel what they would have been without it. For even their complexions could not be ascertained, for their Skins were bismeared with soot and Red ochre.

Probably Frances did not understand that the labret had a status significance for the Tlingit women. Heinrich Holmberg wrote that "As soon as the first signs of maturity appear in a girl her lower lip is pierced and usually a bone point is inserted in the opening, though sometimes silver is used. As long as she remains unmarried she wears this, but when she gets a husband a large ornament of bone or wood which is slightly grooved on the gum side is pressed into the opening. Through the years the ornament is enlarged so that the old women wear them over two inches long."[1] The important point is that the labrets denoted the status of the women and were worn with pride. Slaves were recognizable by the absence of this conspicuous decoration.

The origin of the labret is not known. The ornaments have a fairly limited distribution: parts of the North Pacific coast from Japan to Puget Sound, parts of Central America and south to Peru and the Amazon; there is also a line of labret users across Central Africa. Although they are found in the Gulf of Georgia area in archaeological digs, the use of labrets among the early people of the Salish area was discontinued about 2,000 years ago.

What Frances labelled "dirt" on the faces of the Tlingit women was there for good reasons. Aurel Krause wrote that both sexes painted their faces red and black, using a charcoal of fir pitch, soot or graphite, mixed with seal grease, or a brown powder, made by burning a sponge to charcoal and pulverizing it, or red ochre powdered to make a red cream. The Tlingit said they smeared their faces to protect the skin against the winter cold and the danger of snow blindness, or the radiant heat of the open fire (where the women gathered to cook). In summer a sooty face was protection against the insect plagues, and on long sea voyages the glare from the water was made more bearable. And of course faces were supposed to be painted! Who would think of not painting the face? Holmberg wrote that a wealthy Tlingit painted his face daily. Some modern women would feel "undressed" if their skin and lips were not coloured, and our brilliant lipsticks would make the Tlingit ochre appear pale. Frances Barkley probably had her own creams and ointments for the protection of her English complexion. In Europe at that time women of wealth typically painted their faces white with a dressing containing lead, which proved devastatingly destructive to their skin. Perhaps Frances would have been less upset by the Tlingit "dirt" if she had recognized it as a cosmetic.

Their hair, however, is dark & Shiney, and appeared to be kept in good order, parted in the middley and kept smooth on each side behind the Ears, and tyed at the top in a knot. The Men on the contrary have theirs Matted and daubed with Oil and ochre. The dresses of both sexes is made of the Skins of animals, some tanned with the fur on and some without. The women seldom wear any valuable Furs. The Men sometimes wear the Sea Otter Skins, of which they know the Value of, and will strip themselves when ever they can make a good bargain. The women have sometimes a kind of Rugg thrown over their shoulders, a Manufacture of their own. They wear it over their Skin Dresses. The Men in like manner wear two or more Sea Otter Skins sewed together which they throw over themselves, but not having any tight Dress like the women under neath, their Persons are dreadfully exposed, whereas the Women are very decent & Modest.

The people we saw did not seem settled. They had come on a Fishing expedition we conjectured, and they hastily built up huts with boards with which each Canoe was furnished, upon a small

Island; and when they had sold the few furs they had with them, and had begged and got all they could out of the Ship, they went off, leaving a few Fisher Men, who were very diligent in Catching small Fish, which we bought; and the Women returned frequently with very nice berries of differant kinds, such as Wild Strawberries, Blackberries of differant sorts, not what we know by the Name of Black-berries, which grow on the black Thorn, but a berry resembling a Currant; Rasberries of excellant flavour and considering the difficulty of picking them in such a Wild country, plenti-ful. The Men brought an indifferant kind of Salmon with a long

A Port Mulgrave man wearing a sea-otter robe. Drawn by a Spanish artist.

snout. It might have been out of season. The flesh looked very pale. They likewise brought a few River Trout, very large but the flesh quite white, not the pale pink colour of our Trout.

The only weapon for defence that we saw them with were Spears with large sharp *Iron* barbs at least half a Yard long, of which they seem to possess a great number, and also Daggars which the Men wear suspended round their Necks.

A Tlingit basket given to Frances Barkley in 1792.

I was allowed to Land here often, and Captn Barkley and myself explored the Island which Sheltered and indeed made the Harbour we Lay in, and were astonished to see the traces of Cultivation. The ground was covered with coarse grass but a few Oats amongst it, Peas, one crop apparently just out of bearing and another in bloom, a very few plants of course, but plenty of Strawberry Plants, not of the Wild sort, but evidantly had been planted. They were all stripped of their fruit, no doubt by our Friends, who brought them on board. Indeed all they brought us were dead Ripe but of a good size of the sort we call Carolina.

The Ship having now been put in Order and the Water buts filled, we were preparing for our departure on the 25th when we were surprised by the appearance of a Brigg which hove in sight in the Offing. We pleased ourselves with the idea of seeing some of our Country Men, when we saw a Boat approach and entered the Sound. Captn Barkley went off in order to conduct them into Port, or to render them any assistance they might require, and was astonished and disappointed at finding that there were no Officer on board the Boat, only four Sailors, who said they were dispatched upon seeing a Sail in the Sound to get relief, they being very short of Provisions; that their Vessel which was

an American Brigg, Commanded by a Captain Hancock[2] last
from China; that they were going to try their fortune on the
Coast and were on their way to Prince Williams Sound. The
Brigg was to remain at the entrance of the Sound until they
returned to report their success. These four Men were detained
to take refreshment, being very much exhausted, and when
rested they got on board their Boat again, in order to join their
own Vessel. But no Vessel was to be seen, so that after pretend-
ing to have been rowing about all night they returned, saying the
Brigg must have been blown off the Coast. But as it was a very
fine night Captn Barkley began to suspect that all was not right,
and as the Men appeared able bodied Sea Men, he took them on
board and promised them a passage to China. They were thank-
ful, not as they said much relishing the being left to Winter on
the Coast with Savages. They were without Clothes or provisions
of any kind, so that it had altogether a very odd appearance.

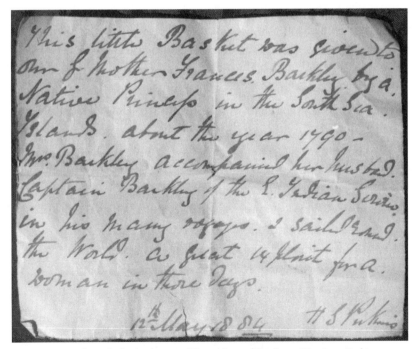

A note written about the basket by one of Frances' granddaughters, Henrietta Perkins,
in 1884.

We remained however three days to give the Vessel an opportunity of returning but as they did not, we set Sail with this addition to our Crew. That they had been turned adrift and deserted, there could be no doubt. We had scarcely got an Offing when on the 29th a violent Wind arose so that we were obliged to stand out to Sea, and when we had weathered the Gale, Captn B. went in the Boat to seek a Harbour, but proved unsuccessful, and the Wind continuing to blow on the Shore, he was obliged to give up his intention of visitng Portlocks Harbour, the Wind being so very unfavourable. But when the weather became more mild he made for Norfolk Sound, where we anchored in a Cove at the Bottom of the Bay. The serounding Country looked very green and pleasant.

The log of the *Halcyon* for Saturday, September 1, 1792, noted: "the first part a strong gale and high seas, running for Cape Edgecumb" and mentioned the breakers on the reef. The entrance is about two miles wide. Once anchored inside the entrance, the captain wrote in the log, "the immense seas … followed us until we rounded the Reef, made it with the night awful beyond description." Frances suppressed any mention of perils or fear.

The day after our arrival brought a number of visitors who came in large well apointed Canoes. They fixed their habitations on the beach opposite the Vessel and displayed several fine Sea Otter Skins, but they set such a high value on them that it was very difficult to deal with them. There was no end to their demands. Powder & shot was always the first demand (arms they had plenty, two or three Muskets in every Canoe) then Blankets, Cooking Utensils and tools, or other Iron weapons with which they are very expert. Indeed, they seemed the most dangerous and mischevious set we had ever Met, and so dilatory in their traffick that, altho there seemed no difficulty in getting a fresh supply, they kept haggleing with what they had, whereby much time was lost. Yet Captn Barkley purchased a pretty good lot.

The Inhabitants increased dayly, and they got so bold and troublesome at last that it became difficult to avoid disputes, stealing every article that they could lay their hands upon, stripping the Men, when they ventured on shore, and upon the slightest offence presenting their fire arms, the use of which they perfectly knew, but they had never felt the effects of them, we conjectured, certainly not of the great Guns. Captn B. upon one or two occasions had them fired off to astonish them, but they only seemed to think him in play. Thank God we left them in ignorance of their deadly effect. But as they saw the Trees shivered, and must have used their muskets in warfare with other Tribes, they must have been awair of what mischief they could do.

Once, in particular, Captn B. saw several War Canoes with his Night Glass, stealing along under the shadow of the land on a fine moonlight Night, and as we were very indifferently Man'd, he was suspicious of their intentions, and therefore he had a whole Broad side fired off over their heads, which made a great noise amongst the trees. We heard them scuttle off, but kept perfect silence on board that they might not think we were alarmed. Early the next morning they came alongside dressed in their War dresses, and singing their War Song & keeping time with their paddles. When they had paddled three times round the Vessel they set up a great Shout, then pulled off their masks and resumed their usual habits, and exhibited their sea otter skins, and gave us to understand they had been on a war expedition and had taken them from their Enemies. They never alluded to the firing, but went on trading as if nothing had passed, firing of their own Muskets in the Air, and then giving a great shout.

They are a very savage race and their women still more frightful than the women of Admiralty Bay, the disgusting Mouth piece being still Larger than theirs. In fact the Mouth piece in the old women were so large that the Lips could not support them, so that they were obliged to hold it up with their hands, and to close their Mouths was a great effort; and when shut the Under Lip entirely hid the Upper one entirely, and reached up to the Nose. That gave them a most extraordinary appearance, but when they open it to Eat, they do not appear like anything. For they are obliged to support the Lip whilst they open their Mouths, and then they through the food into their mouths, throwing back their heads with a jerk to prevent the food lodging in the artificial Mouth or saucer, which is concave and lets down to receive whatever escapes the right chanel. How any rational creature could invent such an inconvenient machine, I am at a loss even to guess, as there is no stage of it that has the most distant appearance of orniment. In the Young Women it looks like a second Mouth as long as the lip will bear its weight.

The women supplyed us regularly with a vast quantity of fresh plucked berries and wild flowers. There was one sort of Berry differant to any one I ever saw. It was of a pale transparent Red colour the size of a Currant but grows seperately like the black Currant on the slender twigs of a very Elegant Bush as tall as a Barberry & Much such a Plant. They brought Bough's & the fruit hanging to it. The fruit was rather tart, but of a delicious flavour. I made some preserve of it, which proved very grateful to us all when we were at sea, and we regaled ourselves with it whilst in our reach. The Strawberries were done, but the other berries were often covered with the leaves of that plant, so that they must be wild in the Woods, altho those we met with in Admiralty Bay must have been cultivated.

The Men did not perform their task, by bringing Fish. They seem very Idle. Now and then a few flat Fish is all we could obtain from them. They seem to think of nothing but their arms, being very proud of their Spears, which are a very formidable weapon, being Similar to those used by the Natives of Admiralty Bay, and they are very expert in the use of them, and say they like them better than Muskets because they are sure to hit, but the fire arms made a great Noise but did not always do execution.

Aided by the Vocabularies annexed to Captn Cooks Narative, Captn Barkley soon understood their meaning, his aptitude in Languages being of an extraordinary nature, to which was joined great perseverance. The language of the Natives of Nootka Sound he perfectly understood, having in our Visit to that part of the Coast in a former Voyage regularly studied it. And the Chiefs Maguilla and Callecum seemed more intelligant beings, but not so

Warlike as these Northern Savages. Still they are more active and enterprising, and if we had stayed a Winter on the Coast, I dare say that should have got an excellant Cargo of Sea Otter Skins; but we began to be short of provisions, in consequence of the extortions in Kamschatka.

I have no memorandum of the time we remained, but the Long-Boat was dispatched from thence, to Captn Portlocks Harbour, and was absent 16 days and returned with one Skin, Mr. Nowell, the Mate who commanded her, having experienced very bad weather. He reported the Sound in which Portlocks Harbour is situated of such vast extent that he did not attempt to explore it. That is the part of the Coast that Captn Barkley was most desirous of Visiting, but as I before observed, we were blown off the Coast, which appears not to be favored with pleasant weather, when we consider that this was the Middle of August.[3] And the fruit we got ripened at a much more advanced season on this Coast than the same berries in England or even in Scotland.

On our former Voyage we found the Climate much Milder, although we had a dreadful storm the day we first made the Coast off Nootka Sound, which was the Northernmost part of the Coast we visited on that expidition; and from thence made excursions to the Southward, a part of the Coast that Captain Cook was prevented visiting by Temtious Weather. And we were consiquently the first Ship that ever at that time had visited a large sound in the Latitude Named it Wickinanish's Sound, the Name given it by the Chief, who seemed to possess great authority there. This part of the Coast proved a rich harvest of furs. Likewise another very large sound to which Captn Barkley gave his own Name, calling it Barkleys Sound, and several coves and Bays he Named. There was Frances' Island, Williams point, and a variety of other Names. There was Hornby Peak, and a variety of familiar appellations, all of which were left out of the plan of the Coast by Sir Josiph Banks, who surreptitiously obtained from Captn Barkley his plans and drawings, and under various pretences retained them.

In the same manner Captain Mears got possession of his journal from the persons in China, to whom Captn Barkley was bound under a penalty of five thousand pound to give them up, for a certain time, for mercantile objects, the owners not wishing the knolidge of the coast to be published. Captn Mears, however, with the greatest afrontery published and claimed the merit of the discoveries therein contained, besides inventing lies of the most revolting nature, tending to vilify the person whom he thus pilfered. No cause can be assigned, except the wish of currying favor with the Agents of the Ship *Loudoun* which was the Ship that Captn Barkley commanded, they, the Agents, having quarelled with him in consiquence of his claiming a just demand. The fact was that he was appointed to the Command of the *Loudoun* and ingaged to perform three Voyages, for which he was to have three thousand pounds. But the Owners being Supercargoes in China in the Service of the East India Service, as well as Directors at home, in the Company's Service, they found that they were not waranted in trading to China, and therefore found themselves obliged to give up and sell the Ship to avoid worse consiquences. They then wanted to get off their contract with Captn Barkley, who, having made provision accordingly would have been actually a loser by the concern himself, after making upwards of ten thousand pounds for the owners, beside loss of time and great expenses incurred in returning to England. He of course brought an action against them for damages, but the affair was compromised by an Arbitration of Merchants, and he was awarded five thousand pound, the whole transaction being the most arbitrary assumption of power ever known. For they not only dismissed him to answer their own purposes, but appropriated all the fittings up and stores laid in for the term agreed for, which would have taken up at least ten years, for he was to winter on the Coast the second and subsiquent Voyages, which was to imbrace the whole of the Coast of America, Kamschatka and the Japan and to open a trade with the unfrequented ports of China, where the Furs were likely to Sell.

Upon his return to Macao, Meares formed a new company called the Merchant Proprietors Company made up of some of his old Bengal Fur

Company associates. Their intent was to send ships back to Nootka Sound the following season and establish a trading outpost, thereby garnering a major hold on the fur trade. It would have been of benefit for Meares to have access to Barkley's charts and navigational instruments. Throughout the history of merchant shipping it has been the practice of masters to supply their own navigational instruments and Barkley's, according to Frances, were of the finest quality.

Of course he had supply'd himself with the most expensive nautical Instruments and stores of every kind, a great part of which he had been obliged to expend upon the owners, who had not laid in sufficient Stores for such a Voyage, and then pretended that he was bound to furnish them, so that they actually brought him apparently in debt to the concern; and it became certain when the affair was investigated that all the articles thus obtained were transferred to Captn Mears, who was in the same imploy, altho not acknolidged to be so. Altho the same objection did not actually subsist with respect to his Vissel that there was to the *Loudoun,* the one having been fitted out in England, and the other in Bengal, so that there was no Law in force to prevent the Company's Servants having a property in her, she being construed what was called a Country Ship, namely a trading Ship from Port to Port in the Indian Seas, whereas the *Loudoun* was actually a Ship which by the Company's Charter was not allowed to go to China from Europe.

This account of the dispute with the owners of the *Imperial Eagle* may be compared with the version in Chapter Five of this book, which was quoted by Walbran directly from Frances Barkley's Diary, to demonstrate the manner in which the Diary served as a source in the writing of the *Reminiscences.*

After her diatribe against the owners of the *Imperial Eagle* and Captain Meares, Frances left six empty pages, failing to write of the progress of the *Halcyon* from Norfolk Sound to the Sandwich Islands (Sitka Sound to Hawaii). From the log it is known that this part of the voyage began on Thursday, October 4, and that Owhyhee (Hawaii) was sighted on Wednesday, November 7, 1792.

HAWAII

Second voyage, in continuation:

We made the island of Oyhee on the 7th of November, after a tedious voyage. As soon as we came in Sight at two or three Miles distance, we were met by several large Canoes with provisions on board, which they were willing to barter for Iron, tools &c, but we find them more difficult to deal with than they were on our first visit.

From a crack in the earth's crust, erupting lava built the submerged mountain range whose eight highest peaks form the chain of lovely islands called

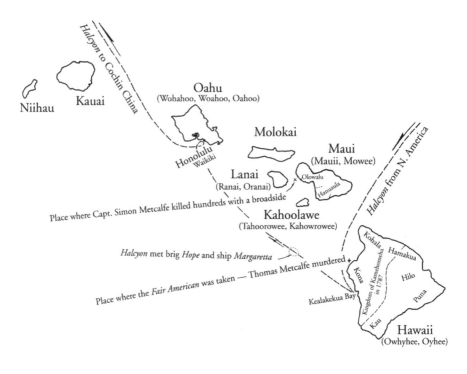

T. Jarvie

The Hawaiian Islands.

the Hawaiian Islands, but which Cook named the Sandwich Islands to honour the Earl of Sandwich, then First Lord of the Admiralty. The highest mountains are on the island of Hawaii, which Frances spelled Oyhee, where the volcanic peaks stretch 4,900 metres into the great dome of sky. Isolated by vast wastes of ocean, these islands lay for long years uninhabited by man, until they were discovered about a thousand years ago by Polynesian seafarers. After the last of the Polynesian arrivals, the ancestors of the historic Alii (the ruling class), the peoples of the Hawaiian Islands lived apart from the rest of the world until the year 1778. In that year their shocked eyes beheld Captain Cook's vessels, the *Discovery* and the *Resolution*, on the western horizon. There was intense excitement. The enterprising islanders were quick to discover that the strangers had iron and guns, both extremely useful in the prolonged power struggle being waged by the king and nobles of the islands. The Hawaiians were eager to get iron (as Frances and Charles discovered) for they had only a few small bits of the metal, probably acquired on driftwood from Japan. Captain Clerke of the *Discovery* wrote: "This is the cheapest market I ever yet saw. A moderate sized Nail will supply my Ships Company very plentifully with excellent Pork for the Day, and as to the Potatoes and Tarrow, they are attained upon still easier Terms, such is these People's avidity for iron."[4]

On his return to Hawaii in 1779, Cook became involved in a dispute concerning the theft of a canoe and was killed on the beach at Kealakekua Bay, on the island of Hawaii. After this tragic event, and the departure of the *Resolution* and *Discovery*, no foreign ships are known to have visited the islands until 1786. It was the development of the fur trade along the northwest coast of America that brought ships back to the Sandwich Islands, a trade which was a direct consequence of Cook's men selling Nootkan furs for high prices in Canton. In 1786 four foreign ships visited the islands: two of them, commanded by Captains Portlock and Dixon, were English, and the other two were French naval vessels under the command of La Perouse. The following year the *Imperial Eagle* reached Hawaii.

Some of the Hawaiians were eager to travel. Perhaps the most distinguished of these early Hawaiian tourists was the high-ranking chief Kaiana, or Tianna, who went with Meares in 1787 and returned to Hawaii in 1788 after visiting China and the northwest coast of North America. He was with Winée when she died aboard Meares' ship. Another traveller was the man

The village of Kaawaioa, on Kealakekua Bay, where Captain Cook was killed.

called Charles who sailed with Captain Vancouver. However, the very first Hawaiian to sail with Europeans and the first to be employed on a foreign ship was Winée, hired as a maid to Frances.

On that first visit in 1787, the Barkleys gave a pair of turkeys to Kamehameha, and in her *Reminiscences* Frances asserted that they thus introduced turkeys to the Hawaiian Islands. It is interesting to discover in the *Reminiscences* how frequently the voyaging explorers planted crops in remote places, so that future travellers would find food. In the next paragraph there is mention of Captain Rogers (of the vessel *Fair Britannia,* from Calcutta in 1791) and his gift of melons. The *Reminiscences* continue:

> In addition to the usual productions of this fertile island we found both March & Water Mellons. They were given by Captn Rogers, who brought the seeds, which have produced a wonderful Crop, and the seeds having been propogated, this cool refreshing fruit is now very abundant. We were afterwards highly gratefied to find Turkeys on the Island which are the produce of a Turkey Cock & hen we left, or rather gave a Cheif five years

ago. They did not, however, bring any for sale. They are too highly prized, and are principally handed from one Chief to another, as a peace offering upon great occasions, Originals have caused a desperate War.

Here we met Tyanna, the Chief that Captn Mears patronised and courted, altho he proved to be a great Rascal, altho held up as a paturn of every excellance by that Gentleman. It was by his information and conivance that a small American schoner commanded by a Young Man of the Name of Medchalf was Cut off, and every Man but one were Murdered. She was badly Manned and never intended to be Sent unprotected to the Sandwich Islands but was fitted out & sent on a trading expedition on the Coast of America, by his Father Captn Midcalf, who was on a trading Voyage; and this young Man was to meet his Father at a given point, but having missed his Father's ship at the place of rendevous, he sailed for the Sandwich islands, in hopes of finding him there, and was unfortunately Cut off. The Schooner was carried into Caracasoa Bay, where she was taken.

The American trader, Captain Simon Metcalfe, had two vessels: the *Eleanora,* and a tiny schooner called the *Fair American,* commanded by his son Thomas. They had been on the northwest coast in 1789, where the smaller vessel had been seized by the Spaniards and taken to San Blas. When released, young Thomas sailed for Hawaii. His father was already there, anchored off Honuaula, Maui, trading for supplies. Captain Simon Metcalfe seems to have been a violent man. When natives stole a small boat tied to the *Eleanora,* killing a sailor on guard, the captain fired rounds of shot into the village, causing the deaths of several villagers. He then sailed to Olowalu to recover the stolen boat, but finding it broken up, he fired a broadside into an assemblage of canoes, slaughtering more than a hundred people. Earlier, he had struck a chief, Kameeiamoku, for some petty offence aboard the *Eleanora,* and the chief had sworn to avenge himself on the first foreign vessel to present itself. This, by chance, was the *Fair American,* whose captain was young Thomas Metcalfe.

Kameeiamoku went aboard the *Fair American,* and easily killed the unsuspecting young captain and all the crew except one, Isaac Davis. This cruel action took place off lands ruled by Kamehameha, a powerful king, who took Isaac Davis under his protection, as well as the *Fair American,* which became part of Kamehameha's fleet. Meanwhile, the *Eleanora* was at anchor in Kealakekua Bay, a few miles south, and when the boatswain of the ship, John Young, went on shore Kamehameha detained him, fearing that if Captain Metcalfe learned of the death of his son, he would wreak vengeance on the villages. However, Metcalfe sailed away without knowing the fate of young Thomas, and Davis and Young stayed with Kamehameha and were given wives, lands, servants and wealth, in effect becoming Hawaiian chiefs and advisors to Kamehameha.

Frances suggests that it was by the instigation of Tianna, the Hawaiian chief who went with Captain Meares and who subsequently became an ally of and advisor to Kamehameha, that the *Fair American* was captured. Certainly it was Kamehameha who profited from the crime. At this time, when the warring factions were resting between wars, the arrival of the foreign ships provided access to new weapons in the armament race. In the spring of the same year, 1789, Kamehameha had obtained arms and ammunition from Captain Douglas (in command of the *Iphigenia Nubiana,* a ship purchased by Meares for his company, the Merchant Proprietors, organized in 1787) as well as a swivel gun which he mounted on the platform of a large double canoe. Frances got her information from Charles, a Hawaiian man:

> We here fell in with a youn Man that had sailed with Captain Vancouver in his Magesty's ship Discovery — he called himself Charles and it was from him we learned the Character of Tyanna, and of his hand in the transaction respecting the Schoner. Charles was a Native of Moratoi, and was only at Oyhee on business. This is the account he gave of himself.
>
> Captn Barkley had intended taking water here, besides provisions, but Charles remonsterated so strongly with him that he agreed to go to Wohahoo, particularly as Charles (who spoke English perfectly well) said that two Vessells had passed the East End of the Island the day before, probably bound for that Island. Indeed, being very badly man'd, it was very desireable to meet with other Vessels, besides which the *Venus* might be one of them.
>
> Accordingly we set all sail, and on rounding the East Point we discryed them, and soon after spoke the Brig *Hope,* Captn

Ingraham, from the Coast of North West America, and afterwards the Ship *Margaretta,* Captn. Maggee of Boston.

Ralph Kuykendall, noted author of *The Hawaiian Kingdom, 1778-1854,* wrote that the American trader Ingraham, believing his small vessel in danger of attack, fired a number of shots to scare off the natives. From the moment of the very first contact with Europeans, before Captain Cook's ships had anchored — when a party was sent toward land in small boats to discover a suitable landing and watering place, and one of the natives was shot and killed by Lieutenant Williamson for apparently trying to take a boat hook — the relationship between Europeans and Sandwich Islanders was one of profound mistrust, with bloody and violent deeds on both sides.

Captn Maghee informed us of the *Venus'* arrival on the Coast of America the latter part of June, and of his having been seen amongst the Queen Charlots Islands by Captain Vancouver, and that Captn Sheapard and all the Crew were well. This was good News. It was agreed between Captn Maghee, Captn Ingraham and Captn Barkley that we should keep Company for mutual security, and accordingly set sail for Whitaty Bay, in the Island of Wohahoo, there to take in water; but the supply of Water was very scanty, and likewise the provisions, compaired with what we should have found had we Anchored in Caracacoa Bay. However, we got a few Hogs, Potatoes, Yams, Sugar Canes, Melons, Plantains, &&c —

At the bottom of the Bay is a very large and beautiful village, situated in a grove of Cocoa Trees, well cultivated grounds and very neat inclosures and large low built habitations, and it seemed thickly inhabited. Not only in the Village, but the whole Island appeared studded with habitations, and in high cultivation, which gave the place such a cheerful appearance that we were greatly pleased with the View. The Canoes, however, were few in number. The only Child I ever saw in any of the Islands was in a Canoe in this Bay. Its head was shaved, and appeared ill favoured and dull.

The women are very bold and forward, but nether so handsome or so clean as the women of Oyhee. Their dexterity in swimming is most surprising. They are quite equal to the men in the Art, and cannot be distinguished from them in the Water; it is a disgusting sight. And both Men and Women have generally Sore Eyes, which detract from their good look. I suppose this affection is owing to the glare of a tropical Sun on the Sea, in which element they pass so much of their time. The Women have no pretentions to beauty, but they are very active and lively, and also healthy. I did not see any vestages amongst them of Leprosy, which we remarked amongst the Men of Awhyhee. We were surprised to find so few articles of curiosity amongst them, but the Feathered Cloaks & helmets are only worn by the Chiefs and the King, who appears to Rule the whole of the group of Islands called by Captn Cook Sandwich Islands. The Kings name when we visited Owhyhee was Tomahomehaw, a perfect savage.

Kamehameha, whom Frances called "a perfect savage," in later years succeeded in defeating his rivals on the island of Hawaii, and finally unified all the islands under his rule, from 1795 to 1819. When Frances met him, he was undoubtedly formidable. On a later visit to the islands, Vancouver wrote of Kamehameha: "I was agreeably surprised in finding that his riper years had softened that stern ferocity which his younger days had exhibited, and had changed his general deportment to an address characteristic of an open, cheerful and sensible mind: combined with great generosity, and goodness of disposition."[5]

Although the remark about Kamehameha is the last sentence in Frances' small notebook of *Reminiscences,* one further piece of her writing survives. Among the Barkley papers in the British Columbia Archives there is an account written by Frances in 1793, describing her visit to Cochin China; it is not known whether this section was a part of the missing Diary. From this important document and from other sources, it is possible to complete an account of the voyage.

The log of the *Halcyon* off Waikiki, states:

Friday, Nov. 9, 1792: "Delivered a letter to one of the Chiefs for Captain Shepherd in case he should touch at this island."

Saturday, November 10: "Captains Maggee and Ingrham came aboard me to supper at 3 PM. We were alarmed by the sight of a fire raft very near us and as our decks were very cumbered with hogs and many things we had purchased and I lie a distance without the other two vessels and the raft seeming to be particularly aimed at me, cut my cable and put to sea. The two American ships followed me. As soon as we could get our guns to bear, we fired several shot both at the raft and the shore where the [indecipherable] disappeared."

Sunday, November 11: "And now that I find so many vessels now in this Trade than I had any idea and that skins are so high on the coast, I think it must be better to go on to China and endeavour not to be the last in the market, since I think it totally impossible for Shepherd to remain another season, both for want of Provisions and more especially Trade, there being such an extraordinary competition and such a quantity as well as variety required that he, I am sure, could have no chance, & would be only incurring another

The last page of Frances Barkley's Reminiscences.

years wages and expense to very little purpose, if the Trade is worth following at all, which I begin to doubt."

COCHIN CHINA

Tuesday, November 13: "At Sunsett I bore away for China in company with the *Hope* Brig, Capt. Ingrham."

Sunday, December 23: "At daylight saw many fishing boats and at 10 AM saw the coast of China."

Monday, December 24: "Got the Boat out and sent her to a Fishing Vessel but could not procure a Pilot, hoist her in again. At 8, saw the Grand Lima and got a Pilot on board. Paid him 30 dollars to carry us to Macao Roads, the weather thick Fogg."

This section of the log of the *Halcyon* ends halfway down the page, and the remainder is blank. The Barkley logbooks in the BC Archives consist of the compilation of sections of the logs of various vessels, including the period in the cruise of the *Halcyon* from Monday, February 25, 1793 (the departure from Macao), to Thursday, June 6 (the arrival at Mauritius). The first entries in the section record daily data for the 11 days between Macao and Cochin China. On March 6 the ship approached Cape St. James, and then anchored in a bay about a mile inside Cape St. Jacques. This section ends, "The Mandarins of the Vigia came off to visit the Vessel. Treated them with some spirituous Liquors." Two empty pages follow. Then the log continues its record, the pages headed by the words, "Brig *Halcyon* from Cochin China towards Mauritius," beginning with a first entry dated March 24, 1793. The 18 days in Indochina would be as blank as the empty pages of the log except for the chance survival of an account written at the time by Frances, recording an adventure which is reminiscent of Mrs. Anna Leonowens' experiences, made memorable in *Anna and the King of Siam*.

Information about Indochina at this time is also available from another source, the account of a visit to Indochina in the same year, 1793, by a British trade mission called the Macartney Expedition. Young John Barrow, who would one day hold a dominant position at the British Admiralty, was, when he wrote *A Voyage to Cochinchina*, an amusing and wide-eyed traveller in a junior position in the prestigious trade mission. Although John Barrow and Frances Barkley had much in common (he lived from 1764 to 1848 and her lifetime was 1769 to 1845) and shared a sharp enjoyment of their separate journeys as well as the ability to record what they saw in lively prose, Barrow's observations were for publication and therefore relate background history.

The boundaries of China 200 hundred years ago were not so very different from those of today. An atlas shows the southern border of China at about latitude 22°N. Along the eastern coast of Asia, the countries the Barkleys found recorded on their charts were Tung-quin, Cochin China, Tsiompa and Cambodia. Barrow wrote that these names were unknown to the natives, except Tung-quin, and that the other three were collectively called An-nan, and were divided into three areas: Don-nai, Chang and Hué. In 1774, almost 20 years before Frances' arrival, the kingdom of An-nan was ruled by Caung-Shung, but in that year there was a sudden and disastrous insurrection, the Tayson Rebellion, in which the rightful king was killed, together with 20,000 other inhabitants of the city of Saigon (Sai-gong). His queen fled to the forest with the crown prince and the crown prince's family, accompanied by a most remarkable French missionary by the name of Adran. The crown prince was soon crowned King of An-nan, taking his father's name, Caung-Shung. While the new king was

Cochin Chinese shipping.

fighting to regain his kingdom, Adran returned to France to seek French military assistance, taking with him the young king's little son, a gentle, shy boy who delighted the court of Louis XVI, and who was Frances Barkley's escort on her visit to the Court of Cochin China. By the time Adran returned with the boy prince, the young King Caung-Shung had already reconquered Don-nai, was established in Sai-gong, and was preparing to carry the war northwards into Chang. Ultimately he would reunite the entire kingdom of An-nan and conquer Tung-quin as well, and would then demonstrate his extraordinary capabilities in peace as well as war, but this later development is not part of the Barkley story.

Frances does not describe the 40-mile passage up the great river of Don-nai to the port city of Sai-gong, but Barrow has preserved for us this picture of the river:

> An English gentleman, on his passage from China to India, represented it to me as one of the grandest scenes that could be imagined. It has several large branches, but the width of that up which they sailed seldom exceeded two miles, and in many places was less than one; but the water was so deep in every part, that the rigging of their vessel was sometimes entangled in the branches of the stately forest trees which shaded its banks, and her sides frequently grazed against the verdant shores.[6]

Unfortunately, Barrow did not name the "English gentleman," who could have been Charles Barkley. Barrow wrote that Caung-Shung had refortified the devastated city of Sai-gong and was building a fleet with which to attack the strongholds to the north, and Frances gives a graphic description of the military activities in this area. She wrote:

> Saturday 9th of March 1793
> Notwithstanding the badness of the Boat on which we were embarked, we reached Binga or Sogon, the presant Capital of Cochin China, by two o'clock the next day, being exactly twenty four hours from the time we left Cape St. James, a distance of 23 or 24 Leagues, having besides been detained during that interval two hours at the custom house and nearly six hours waiting for the tide,

which nothing but absolute necessity will induce the natives to stem. At spring tides it runs at the rate of four or five miles pr hour.

As we did not chuse to take up our residence on shore, being ignorent of the kind of accomodation we were likely to meet with, we accepted Mr. Gumbou's invitation on board of the Brig Mary belonging to him, lying opposite the City, where we were most hos-pitably entertained by

Cochin Chinese man.

the Captain, who very politely gave us the use of his Cabin & every accomodation we could desire. As the Vessel was anchored close to the shore, we commanded a view of the whole of the Town as well as of the King's Palace, which thus seen makes a very handsome appearance, not that of a single Palace, but a Citadel of considerable extent, situated rather at the back of the Town with a very long, handsome street (at least half a mile in length) perfectly in a straight line & of a good Width, planted with a double row of Mango Trees, which will, when grown, add much to its beauty. At presant they are but young. The citadal is will provided with Guns. There are two hundred mounted, but as they are all covered by a shed which is built over each to protect them from the sun, they do not make a formadable appearance. Viewed at a distance, the Ramparts are built of Earth inclosed with or faced with Wood, very thick and about 30 feet above the level of the River. The Out Works and Sheveux de Frize are not yet finished. It is sirounded by a very deep Ditch. The Arsanal is within the inclosure & is well found in Amunition and stores of every kind, as well as provisions of all sorts in case of a siege. There is likewise a very Elegant Foundery for Brass Cannon, of which they have in store a great number of amazing size and Bore — not less it is said than two thousand of diffirant sizes, besides swivels and other Armes fit for the Fleet, Muskets etc. for his soldiers. It is likewise provided with work shops for all kind of mechanic's Forges for Iron tools, so that all kind of work is carried on emmidiatly under the King's inspection, whose Palace is in the Center of a prodigious square, which is divided into four equal parts by roads planted with Trees, each leading to a Gate of the Palace, which is Built in the Fashon of the Country very large & Roomy, but not magnificient. Indeed it is said to be only a temporary building suited to the unsettled state of the country, which has been until within these three years divistated by a Civil War, which the presant King has been so fortunate as to overcome, and is now adknoledged the Lawful King by all parties. He has fought hard for it and been a Captive several times.

The French pretended to assist him and did fit out four Frigates of forty guns each to favor his cause, but they came to late so that their suport was ineffectual, which accounts for his priffering the useful insignea of War to the Luxeries of Peace. He is a most astonishing Man, indifatigul in his differant occupations. He superintends all the works carried on for the defence of his Country. His Fleet surpasses anything in this part of the World, both for eficientcy and Beauty. His Galleys are superbe, costly and formidable. They are lay'd up each in a seperate dock & covered in like manner with the Guns in the Fort.

On the morning after our arrival, we had an invitation to spend the day on shore with the french Missionary & other french inhabitants of the City, but as the company was composed intirely of gentlemen I declined the invitation. Capt. Barkley went alone, & I was amusing myself with viewing the scene around me when I percieved a handsome prow come on board and to my great astonishment, I found it brought on board a deputation of Europeans, who came to invite me on shore by the Kings Command, to visit the Ladies of his family in the Palace. I did not at first like to venture so intirely amongst straingers, but the gentlemen having assured me it was a high favor to be thus complimented, and that every preparation was made on shore to receive me with respect, and being allowed to take my little boy with me, a child of ____ years old, I took my seat with Capt. B. and the other gentlemen in the boat, which soon landed us; & we found one of the Kings Palanquins ready to recieve me guarded by at least twenty attendants with Whips and other weapons to keep off the Crowd that had assembled to see the first European Woman that ever visited their country. I had likewise a guard of soldiers who followed, with a band of music, which, together with the noise of the multitude, made such a discordant noise as to terrifie me so much that I was so overcome that it was with difficulty that I could walk, when I was handed from the Palanqueen by the Kings son, a lad about 14 who had been with the French Bishop Adrian to Paris a short time before, to solicit assistance from the King of France.

A type of palanquin, in which Frances Barkley was carried to the Cochin Chinese court. Drawn by J. F. Whittingham.

This young Prince was habited in the most costly manner. He wore a dress peculiar to the next heir to the Throne, he being the Eldest son. It was more like a Persien habit than Chinese, a sort of Tunic of rich Brocade, very stiff, with hanging sleeves imbroidered with gold on a Yellow ground. The imbroidery on the Breast represented a Dragon and the other part was covered with all sorts of hidious figures & Chinese, I suppose, characters. Besides this he wore a vest with what appeared stiff Kings attached to the sholders. It was botton'd with a gold botton at the throat. The tunic was not fastened round the Middle but hung from the neck down to the feet, & stood off as if made of paste Board, so that he appeared as if in a case. He wore sandles on his feet and a very neat Bonnet on his head. He is a very Pretty Boy, and attemted to acost me in the European fason, repeating a few sentences of French, but he seemed very bashful. He conducted me through several apartments, the furniture of which 1 was too much fluried to examine, until we reached the one in which the King's Mother, his Sister & Wife sat ready to recievc me.

They were seated upon a sort of platform, at the uper end of what might be termed a Chamber of Audiance, there being no other furniture in the Room except a rich Carpet spread upon this Platform, which was furnished with rich satun cushons imbroidered with figures like Dragons and other grotesque figures. They were squatted in the Asiatic fashion and had nothing to recommend them in appearance. The Mother was an elderly Woman. She might be sixty, not at all stately in her manner, altho I percieved the other two paid her great respect, and as I aproached the place on which she sat, which was raised three steps above the floor, they spoke in a hurried manner to the young man who was leading me up the steps, & motioned me to a stool that had been previously placed for me, below what I must now Call the Throne.

Besides the Young Prince I was accompanied by what they called an interpreter, who, however, understood so little French, and I so little Porteguese, that I fear their questions were but badly answered; for besides the ignorance of the Man, he was so frightened that he would scarcely speak, and Prostrated himself upon the floor at every sentence in the most ridiculous Manner. We could therefore only satisfie our curiosity by Viewing each other. They spoke amongst each other aparently with great ease & good humour, caressed my little William, who made his way up to them without ceremony & began playing with their betel Boxes and other Toys that were lying about.

They seemed quite pleased with him, examined his hair, his dress & stroked his face, seemed to admire his complection, and by their jestures I conjectured they admired my hair, and seemed to be surprized that my hair should Curl, his being straight. The young Prince, who stood on the first step, was frequently called upon for an explination of that & other parts of my dress, which must have appeared very symple to them, being nothing more than a white Bengal/Muslin Dress with a broad China Ribbon Sash, which is now the fashion, the ends reaching the ground, and the dress has a long train which must have appear'd odd to them who wears everything short, not lower than the Ancle & not make up in any particular fashion, being long pieces of Muslin or Cloth wraped round them fantastically. Altho the Ladies now presant had on vests of brocaded stuff much like Kincob, but upon the whole their appearance did not excite any particular respect, which account for little William's cordiality. He had been used to play with his Indian Nurses in Bengal, who all sit on the floor on Mats.

The Kings Wife is of course Younger than the other two, but she had but a small portion of beauty to boast. In fact, they appeared to me more like Malay women than Chinese. Their complection of a dark Yellow coulour with high Cheek bones, and black teeth. Their manners, however, seemed cortious. They had a small table placed before me on which was served Coffee, sweetmeats & fruits. I heard during my visit a confused murmer & upon looking round I saw that the apartment was divided by a screen, and I afterwards heard that the King & the Males, as well as the other females of his family, were assembled behind it.

I remained in the painful situation above discribed about half an hour, and had some difficulty in persuading my little boy to quit the throne. He was so delighted with roling and tossing about upon the fine cushons. When we got out, which we did in the same manner and with the same din of noise which they called Music, I was in hopes all was over, but without consulting my inclination, I was carried round the City to the houses of some of the principal people belonging to the Court, at each of which I was entertained in the same manner as at the Palace, the principal Lady remaining squatted on a Carpet on the floor at the upper end of the appartment into which I was introduced. Their dress differed very little from the Queens, except that I percieved they wore drawers and a sort of close dress confined at the waist with a sort of sash, bound round very loose and parts of it hanging down like a petticoat. All that I saw in these houses were Old Women. The Young ones I presume were behind the Skrien, which Skrien seemed to be composed of bambo. The Apartments are very dark, the light being admitted at the side, which is shaded generally by a varanda made in a sloping shape which excludes the light materially. I saw but little furniture in any of the roomes. The Ceilings were of a Conical form high in the center and ornimented with carved work & lacred wood —

MAURITIUS

Leaving Cochin China in March of 1793, the Barkleys sailed to Mauritius. Since the time of their first visit there, Port Louis had seen a major increase in shipping from Europe and North America. From 1785 to 1810 almost 600 ships from the United States alone called in at Mauritius. However, when the Barkleys arrived, England and France were at war, yet again. Between 1793 and the signing of the Peace of Amiens in 1802, the French had taken 3,120 British ships. The fighting was very much present in the Indian Ocean where the main subject of conflict was India. Mauritius, a strategic location and entry point to the Indian Ocean, became the port of call of the French naval forces, and the Barkleys sailed innocently into their stronghold.

Some events from the disastrous conclusion of the second voyage are recorded by Walbran, others by Constance Parker. "From private letters and other sources" Walbran wrote:

At Mauritius the French having re-occupied the island, the *Halcyon* with her cargo was confiscated and Capt. Barkley and his crew made prisoners. Through the kindness of an influential merchant named Hippolyte, who received as his guests Capt. Barkley and Mrs. Barkley at his country home on the island, the brig was restored to him. A cargo was found for her, and she sailed for the United States under the charge of an American captain who had been engaged by Capt. Barkley. This man ran away with her, but strange to say, some few years afterwards, when Capt. and Mrs. Barkley were in England, the former received information that his brig *Halcyon* was in Boston. He proceeded to that port and through the influence of the British consul and others who became interested in the case, the brig *Halcyon* once more became the property of Capt. Barkley.[7]

Constance Parker's version differs somewhat. Leaving Cochin China, the Barkleys:

now sailed through the Straits of Singapore, intending to go to Bombay, but were driven too far south, and being ignorant of the fresh outbreak of hostilities between England and France, decided to put into Mauritius for food and water, only to find themselves captives and the *Halcyon* a Prize of War! They were kept a year there and eventually released on parole, and the only way to return home being to ship in an American sailing vessel, the *Betsy,* to Newport by the Cape of Good Hope to the Atlantic. From Newport they got to New York. There Capt. Barkley with the remains of his fortune bought and fitted up the *Amphion* and probably the cargo was cotton, and prepared to sail home. But again was dogged by ill fortune as he found that not being an American citizen he was not allowed to leave the country without an American sailing Master, so had to take one. Started early in November, arriving at Poole Harbour, Dorsetshire, Dec. 1794. Being anxious to take his wife and child to Devonport, Capt. Barkley left the *Amphion* in charge of the sailing master whilst he took them by

coach to London, intending to land the cargo on his return. However, on returning after a short absence he found the rogue of a
sailing Master had gone off with the *Amphion* and all the cargo and
all their things. Not daunted he at once set out to seek him, first in
the dutch ports and then over the Atlantic, where he finally came
up with him in the Brig, but all the Cargo sold. This second voyage
lasted 4 ½ years. Instead of complaints and grumbles, all the hardships and dangers seem to bring out the fine courageous, cheerful
and strong character of Mrs. Barkley and her absolute devotion to
her "beloved husband" as she always calls him, and I think we may
well be very proud of this young great grandmother and of her
husband. Copied by me, 1913. Constance Parker of Waddington,
great grand daughter of Mr. and Mrs. Charles Wm. Barkley and
daughter of John Trevor Barkley by his wife Jane, eldest daughter of
Edward Stanley Esq. of Ponsonby Hall, Cumberland.

It had been a long and perilous voyage. Leaving England early in 1790 in
the *Princess Frederica* for India, then in the *Halcyon* to Kamchatka and Alaska,
the Hawaiian Islands, China, Cochin China, and finally their capture at
Mauritius, in the *Betsy* to Newport, returning to England in the *Amphion* in
November of 1794, they had travelled for four and a half years. It is not
surprising that Frances, Charles and the boy William were eager to leave the
Amphion at Poole, to be with friends and family at Christmas.

With the Cochin China fragment and the brief accounts in Walbran and
Parker, the chronicle of the travels of Frances Barkley ends. What became of
her? The rest of her life was spent in England. A few letters preserved by her
descendants make it possible to have some glimpses into the years from 1794
until Frances' death in 1845, and provide a last chapter for the story.

Chapter Eight
The Barkleys in England

ecember 1794 ... by coach to London! Jolting over the ruts on their way to surprise their relatives at Christmas, returning to safety and comfort after all the years of adventuring, Frances and Charles and six-year-old William must have been in high spirits, quite unaware that their ship and cargo were being stolen and that Charles would spend the next few years searching for the *Amphion*. When the theft was discovered, Frances was probably left to visit relatives, perhaps with Uncle William at Sunbury, or with brother-in-law John Barkley and his wife Elizabeth at Bath, or with one of Frances' sisters or half-brothers.

A granddaughter, Frances Jane Barkley, was to write from Hethersett, Norwich, in 1913, "I remember my Grandmother (a Trevor) as I spend some weeks with her when I was about six years old (and very lame) at Hastings and at Brighton. She would amuse me sometimes with the story of her being, with my Grandfather, prisoners in the Isle of France. Was not [indecipherable] some of her sons, older than your grandfather, were born and died there. The French governor was very kind to them and made great friends with them. She spoke rather funny English from having been brought up in a French convent and she was most gracious and kind but a very violent temper! — She and my grandfather made many voyages together and she was the first Englishwoman who was seen in Vancouver's Islands and in the Coast of British Columbia where Barkley Sound was named after my Grandfather. They had no settled home I think after."[1]

Their lack of a settled home in England has made it difficult to trace their movements.

When Frances returned to England in 1794 she learned that her father had died in January of that same year. Soon after her return, her daughter Jane was born, but Frances waited five years for the birth of a second son, John Charles. In the same year that John Charles made his appearance, 1800, Frances' sister-in-law, Elizabeth Willis Barkley, died at Bath, and as Elizabeth Willis' life and death concerned Frances, who ultimately inherited her wealth, perhaps her story should be briefly told.

Elizabeth Willis was first married to Charles Barkley's uncle, Andrew Barkley, oldest of the three Barkley brothers who had left Cromarty so many years earlier. Andrew, a post captain in the Royal Navy, and the owner of a fine house in Bath, had no children. A chiselled marble memorial to him in Bath Abbey also records the deaths of the two people most closely associated with him:

Sacred to the memory of
Andrew Barkley Esq. late a
Post Captain in the Majesty's Royal Navy
who departed this life January 30th, 1790
Aged 49 years
He married Elizabeth Willis
one of the Daughters of Richard Willis of Digswell
in the County of Hertford, esq. deceased,
who out of respect to the memory of her most
affectionate Husband has caused this Monument
to be erected.
Also of Elizabeth relict of the above named
Andrew Barkley Esq.
Also of John Barkley Esq. his Nephew
who died 16th December 1822, Aged 74 years

The memorial plainly indicates the respect of Elizabeth and the affection of Andrew, but what it does not reveal is that nephew John Barkley then married his aunt Elizabeth. Another Barkley descendant has left us this further comment: "Pretty wealthy ... John B ... I read his long will at Somerset

House some years ago, when I also came across a curious deed by his Aunt Elizabeth executed on the eve of her marriage with John. She describes her parentage, whose widow she is, and who John is, and her lawyer brother-in-law Wm. Barkley of Hartford was party to the transaction."[2] It would seem that the Barkleys took steps to see that Andrew Barkley's wealth stayed in the family, and as Elizabeth Willis had no children in either marriage, Charles and Frances ultimately benefitted.

Andrew Barkley.

The two brothers, John and Charles, had a close relationship throughout their lives, dominated by John, who was 11 years older than Charles. John was wealthy, first from his own career in the East India Company and next from marrying his aunt Elizabeth; he also appears to have inherited Sunbury from Uncle William Barkley. Charles, on the other hand, was poor, the first venture on the *Loudoun* having made little money for him and the subsequent enterprise to the northwest coast of North America being equally unsuccessful financially. It appears that Charles was dependent on John until John's death. The business which might have made Frances and Charles independent, the "country trade" in India, had been disparaged by John, who considered it an unsuitable occupation, and it was at this time that Frances called John their "evil genius" and spoke of his pride.

Charles was like a son to his older brother, who had no children of his own, and Charles and Frances and their children probably lived with John. Certainly Frances was in the Princes' Building home in Bath in May of 1808, eight years after the death of Elizabeth Willis, when she received a letter from Charles, who was travelling with his brother John in Ireland. The letter Charles wrote to his "dearest Fanny" from Dublin casts a bright, warm light on the family. He writes about each child in turn: Jane, John, Patty and "our

The Princes' Building, Bath, the home of the Barkleys. Drawn by J. F. Whittingham.

dear Babe." Jane had been born in the year after the Barkleys returned to England, 1795, and John Charles arrived five years later. In 1802, Frances and Charles lost their oldest son, William Hippolyte Andrew, aged 14, born at Mauritius, and in the year of William's death the second daughter Martha (Patty) was born. "Our dear Babe," Charles Francis, had arrived shortly before his father's departure for Ireland.

> My dearest Fanny,
> I have this instant received your very kind and welcome letter of Friday. You will receive about the same time mine of same date from Holy Head. I am quite delighted to find my Dearest Jane continues to mend. The Shower Bath will, no doubt, do good, but you must not bathe John any longer if it makes his head ache

pretty fellow. Don't continue the bath until you have given him opening medicine. Indeed my love his ear must be attended to. If chance should bring Sherwin in the way make a point of seeing him again, if the Bath makes his head ache or he is feverish he must not take it. Am very glad Dear Patty is so well and our dear Babe's innoculation going on so well. Is it much inflamed? Pray take care of yourself, my dear Fanny. You must not sacrifice yourself. I hope in your next to hear you are better and John's headache removed. Do not push him too hard in study if his head complains. He will be as forward as other boys. He is naturally clever. Health is everything. My sisters letter is welcome in every way and I do not doubt Mr. James will prove a good Tenant. They appear Genteel people. My Brother will take care of Mrs. Holt's commission and desires to be kindly remembered to her if you see her and to Mrs. Lambert.

We arrived here on Saturday at four in the evening. The Tide was out when we came off the bar, and we were put into a small boat to carry us up to Pidgeon House, a strong place on a long narrow Causeway that extends near three miles in length and where the principal depot of Arms is kept. It has 42 pounders directed along the Causeway and is otherwise completely surrounded by the sea, which ebbs from its sides at low water. It is built of stone. About a quarter of a mile without it on the same narrow Causeway stands a neat low light house. The view from it of Dublin Bay is grand and extensive. Here you see several Martello Towers on different commanding points. The Wicklow Mountains on the south add greatly to the scene. They are very high and add greatly to the beauty of the landscape about Dublin.

We were becalmed all night on our passage; otherwise the run is about ten hours with a moderate breeze. The Packets are very fine ones, the same as you have seen at Ostend. Apropos, have you heard from Hannah? If you have not, pray write again. I shall be seriously uneasy for the fate of my other post paid letters until I am convinced she has received the one I wrote her. Have you not yet received what I wrote for, for you, pray my Love say in your next.

We do not like Dublin. Everything is intolerably dear and the streets very dirty. Very few well dressed people passing in the streets, especially women. The old Cathedral of St. Patrick tumbling down, neglected, and to wade through mire of the vilest description to go near it. I am acquainted with the vicinity already, the Post Office, Bank, College; St. Stephen's grass is the largest square I ever saw. I cannot say much in favour of its elegance. There are rows of trees imperfect, a Ditch that smells very badly, within the low stone wall that surrounds a large square field, in the middle, which gives it a little air of a fortified place. The street is wide and the houses some good, some very shabby. There are barracks on one side of the square. Altogether it appears like a place that has been pretty.

Marian Square is very large and would be handsome if the bricks the houses are built of were good. They are of a peculiar colour that gives it a very dismal inelegant look and one universal maxim reigns through the whole city: never to wash or clean the steps before the doors, or pave, which is disgusting. Never, I may say, are they refreshed with sweeping or washing. It is truly very dirty.

The Custom House and keys are very elegant and several ships lying in the river, which is about 200 yards wide at most. There was a general review of the Volunteers yesterday. My brother was too ill to walk. We went in a Hack to see them. They made a grand display (the light horse) kept the ground. We did not see a dozen private carriages. We saw the Lord Lieutenant's house in the Phenix. It is a neat place, nothing Grand about it, and the Castle resembles the inside of the Tower of London, but far smaller.

I must leave off description to tell you my brother has had all his Complaints return again. He kept his bed from Saturday evening 5 o'clock until Sunday forenoon. He has them badly now. I persuaded him to anoint, with Camphorated Spirits and Laudanan. It has relieved him. He desires best love to you all. I have been very unfortunate in my enquires after Mr. William Godfrey. No one knows anything about him but we are going, indeed we are waiting for a gentleman to introduce us to a professional man of high respectability who has engaged to pursue legal measures, so in my next you may expect to hear further. My own opinion is once the affair is committed to Mr. Furlong's management and he is made thoroughly acquainted with the business, we shall return, my brother's stay not being likely to do any good. I have taken inendable pains to enquire everywhere and of everybody. He is alive I see by the Calendar. I have not a doubt but we shall leave Dublin during the course of the week. I shall let you know in time.

My Brother intends staying a day or so at Monmouth on his return, so that you may have occasion to write me to the Post Office there. You will hear from me about that. My Dearest love I wish we were back again. Everything here is intolerably dear and extravagant, much dearer than even Bath. Mutton 9d, beef the same, butter 18d. I am charmed with some parts of Wales, the Rocks stupendous, the roads terrific, the chasms, the deep valleys, all striking you at once, with dread and amazement. Such scenery cannot be described, the awful, the sublime, shifting every two or three miles. Shrewsbury I find is tolerably cheap, mutton 5d, butter 11d, veal 8d, beef 6d. Coals as at·Bath. It is a very large and elegant place and moderate for living. Bangor and Beaumaurice Bay and view of the sea devine. Salmon 6d a pound. Other articles of living very cheap. The Vale of Langollen incomparably fine. I cannot do justice to some things I have seen, but I wanted you and my dear Jane, John and Patty, all of you to allow me to enjoy it. You would have been charmed, especially at Bangor ferry. The country is enchanting, the sea, the fishing boats, the hills behind you, but we are tired of Dublin and wish to quit it as soon as possible. My brother desires you will tell Jane to send immediately to Henry about the pavements and let him do what is necessary about it.

I could say much more about Wales, but have no room. I must now repeat my anxiety for your cough as well as my dear John's ear, but they never can have a better guardian of everything than their dear kind and tender Mother, who will I am sure do everything that is proper and prudent. I most heartily wish to be back. I have no pleasure whatever in being away, especially with the possibility there is of my being away very long which my Brother constantly repeats is not his wish, but that is a joke. I cannot, all things considered, do otherwise. Kiss my Dear Children. Assure them of my tenderest love, and my dearest Fanny with a thousand tender and fond wishes for our speedy meeting, believe me,

Your most affectionate husband

Charles William Barkley

Tell the dear children if I can find anything worth accepting I shall take it to them. Jane some real Limerick Gloves. Shoes are cheap here 8s a pair, that is, cost 13s in Bath.

To Mrs. Barkley, Princes Bldg. Bath.[3]

This letter sheds a new light on the man whom Frances described as a martinet at sea: here is revealed the observant traveller and affectionate husband and father. The infant Charles has just been vaccinated. As it was only in 1798 that Edward Jenner perfected his method of preventing smallpox with a vaccine of cowpox, Frances and Charles were among the first progressive and courageous parents who were taking the risk of having an infant vaccinated. In 1806, two years earlier, London had recorded a most unusual event: one full week without a single death from smallpox. This remarkable achievement was the result of Jenner's work, following Parliament's support in 1802, when money was voted for the improvement and advertisement of his methods.

Charles and his brother John seem to have been in Dublin in search of a Mr. William Godfrey, but it is not clear whether this is the ship's master who stole the *Amphion* 14 years earlier. "I have no pleasure whatever in being away very long, which my Brother repeats is not his wish, but that is a joke." The complex relationship among older brother John, younger brother Charles and his strong-willed Frances is here revealed, for Frances and Charles were much indebted to John. In a letter written a few years later, Charles expressed his gratitude to John: "Without you, my family and me must long ago have felt the severe hand of want."[4]

The Dublin letter is also interesting in the expression of the new Romantic passion for nature; only a man of the time of Wordsworth and Coleridge would write, "Such scenery cannot be described, the awful, the sublime ..."

Two years later, in 1810, Charles made a journey alone to Cromarty in Scotland, to be with his dying cousin James Forbes, the man who had given Charles and Frances such a warm welcome in Calcutta. James Forbes had sent for Charles, his first cousin and closest friend, but the messages had been blocked by relatives who wished to inherit James' wealth. "Miss B." (probably Barkley) from Cromarty "showed some strangeness when Eneas was going on reading his sister's letter."[5] Eneas Barkley ("E.B." in many of the letters) is the villain of the story, as it would appear that his grandfather had wrongfully inherited the Barkley estate named Shingleside. As the evidence in the letters is one-sided, it is impossible to

James Forbes.

judge whether or not there was a miscarriage of justice. In any case, at the time of his journey to be with James Forbes, Charles Barkley was totally unaware that he may have been deprived of his Scottish inheritance.

The letters from Cromarty were addressed to Mrs. Barkley, at Jno Barkley's Esq., Sunbury, Middlesex. Sunbury was the home of Uncle William Barkley, barrister of the Middle Temple, who had died eight years earlier, apparently leaving the Sunbury house to Charles' brother John. The first letter is from Bridlington, a seaport halfway up England's eastern coast, into which Charles' dangerously overloaded packet had sailed for respite from the terrible storm raging across the North Sea: "the most abominable trip I ever undertook ... After the Vessel was crammed full in every part, Cabin and Deck, we took in twenty-one passengers and their luggage ... Fortunately my recommendation from Mr. E. B. has procured me marked attentions from Mr. Clarke, who is a very able and good sailor and good Pilot, and his Smack a very strong one. But such filth never was seen ... The smell is intolerable, from various causes produced by so many people confined together in so small a space." Charles wrote of his uncertainty about the journey: "In fact, my dear Fanny, it is a most awkward undertaking both as to the mode of performing it and the object of it. I cannot positively define whether Forbes has ever been so ill as represented."[6] This letter from Bridlington was written on August 17.

The next letter was written from Cromarty on the 23rd of the month, at two o'clock in the morning, from James Forbes' bedroom in the house belonging to a cousin, Miss Forsyth. Charles reported, "Our friend Forbes is alive, and that is all I can say ... He was very glad to see me and said he wished very much to see me, as he wanted to make a material alteration in his Will. I proposed his doing it immediately with as much delicacy as I could, but he said he should defer it until morning. God knows whether he will be alive for he is in a most deplorable way, yet he is perfectly sensible."[7]

James Forbes lived only two more days, but he survived long enough to execute the codicil to his will, in which he divided his wealth into six shares. The beneficiaries were Charles' brother John, Charles, James Forbes' illegitimate son Robert, William Forbes of Edinburgh (probably a brother), Mary Hunt and her brother (one share between them) and Charles and Frances Barkley's four children (one share). Charles wrote this news to Frances on the 24th, almost as soon as the ink was dry on the codicil. He said he was "very fatigued with attending. There is only his man and me, and he has been constantly wanting shifting the same as a child. Just now there is a little interval, seemingly from nature being quite exhausted. It is a most painful and melancholy task that I have undertaken but I shall perform it as a sacred duty. He, poor soul, seems very highly grateful for my attention and coming down ... There certainly has been some manouvering. It seems he wrote expressly for me to come down by the mail but we were not informed of it ... Be that as it may, I am here, in a most amiable family and what is more they really are our relations. Their grandmother and our grandmother were Morrisons and Sisters. They behave like such. I never met with such Courtesy. They appear to be very pleased at serving me, having long wished to see some of us. They are highly well bred, have a very fine house, are quite without ceremony ... How is it we never knew this before. Miss B., if she had pleased might have explained it."[8]

On August 27, Charles wrote to tell Frances that James Forbes had died. "Every sigh, every groan passed before my eyes to the last gasp ... He would not let my hand go one minute night or day. He was overjoyed when I arrived. He had positively written for me to come down to him immediately by the Mail in a letter to Highbury thro' one of the Miss Barkley's ... Every one here says he spoke of me in raptures, poor fellow ... "[9] By the 29th James Forbes had been buried and Charles prepared to leave Cromarty. He wrote a few lines to Frances, repeating his praises for the new-found relatives: "I have already said much of the family I am living with, too much I cannot say. Their kindness is unbounded, unaffected, unassuming, dignified and courteous."[10] He also sent greetings from the Barkleys of Shingleside, unaware that they may have stolen this fine estate from him. In Edinburgh on September 5, Charles visited William Forbes before setting off in the mail coach for York. The Edinburgh letter concluded the series, without unravelling the mysteries Charles had only glimpsed. Further evidence must have appeared, for a journey to Cromarty was made 23 years later, in 1833, a year after Charles William's death, by his oldest son, John Charles Barkley, who went to Cromarty to investigate his claim to his great-grandfather's estate. It appears that James Barkley's brothers had taken possession of Shingleside and now the former Miss Forsyth had joined with the Shingleside Barkleys to prevent young John Charles Barkley from discovering any firm evidence.

In a letter to his mother, John writes about the difficulties he encountered in the matter of discovering title.

> Cambridge, August 29, 1833
> My Dearest Mother,
> I returned home quite safe after my very long journey on Saturday last. I reached Cromarty on Sunday morning, the 18th and immediately set to work making enquiries which, though they produced no information likely to be of any use in the recovery of the property, tended to confirm the truth of the property having been unjustly alienated from the real owners. Every person whom I questioned admitted that they had always understood the property to be in wrong hands, but none of them could tell me how or what time it had been so alienated ... There cannot be a doubt but that all traces of their family in registers inscriptions and tombstones etc. etc. have been destroyed purposely to frustrate inquiry into the case ... I had repeated interviews with the Schoolmaster and clerk of the Church, and searched the registers, etc. but could

find no trace of any of the name of Barkley previous to the marriage of Mr. Forbes Mother, who was my Grandfather's sister. There is living in Cromarty a common stone mason named Hugh Miller, a self educated young man, who has published a volume of poetry, a history of the herring fishery, and also a history of the antiquities of Cromarty. I had a long interview with him and found him a most sagacious, intelligent and upright man. He said that his attention had been excited to the history of the family from the very circumstance of the absence of all traces of them in the records of the place, tho' it was notorious they were about the oldest inhabitants in Cromarty. He said he had heard it always said that the present branch held the property wrongfully. He had searched every local source of information, hunted over every tombstone, but could find nothing to throw light on their history, and had given it up as a vain attempt. I have engaged him to renew his search, and to communicate with me by letter ...

Hugh Miller appeared to take quite an interest in the matter, and as it jumps with his favorite hobby, I expect some farther information from him. Now the great gap seems to be (and is) between the possession of the property by my Great Grand Father and its coming into the hands of Gilbert Barkley's brother. Annie Barkly seems to have been quite cut out of it as well as her brothers. Her being "Daft" and her husband "no canny" afford some clue to this part of (the affair). I think Hugh Miller will clear this up somehow. It seemed to strike him strongly. "These Barkly's, he said, had certainly nothing to do with Cromarty in those days." I do not expect much, even to gratify my curiosity on the subject, but we shall see ... You must write immediately that I may know how to act.

Believe me,
my dearest Mother,
Your very affectionate son,
J. C. Barkley

Apparently Charles and Frances Barkley's children took no further action concerning the ancestral lands of Shingleside.

One further letter of Charles Barkley's has been preserved, written to his brother John, undated but possibly in 1809. It is a lengthy letter, written from Buenos Aires, where Charles had just resigned the command of the *Venus,* a "very decayed and ill found" vessel in port for repairs. Charles was unwell, full of apprehension about his position, and suffering from an accident ("I fell off the very ladder that did you so much mischeif, as I was going on the poop one night, &

John Charles Barkley.

struck ... against the Traverser of the Charonade.") Charles explained why he undertook the voyage: "Honestly, Dearest Brother, permit me to remark that I was living comfortably with you when this voyage was proposed to me. You was always averse to it. I persevered, pleased with the Idea of getting some hundred pounds both by a little adventure, which you provided me the means of laying in, and by a remuneration for the voyage which latter inticing object required very much more consideration than I bestowed it ... nothing could have induced me to leave a Brother I have so much reason to love, where I was so happy, to go and contend with Climates & privations, which neither my Health nor age are very well able to contend with, for so long a voyage, but to gratify a sense of Duty, & get a little money from my own Labour, since it could in nowise diminish the degree of patronage & protection we with so much Confidence look up to you for ..."[11]

Charles' brother John Barkley died at Bath in 1822, at the age of 74, and the money Charles and Frances inherited may have purchased the fine new house in Hertford. The date of the Barkleys' move to Hertford is not known, but Charles Barkley is listed in Pigot & Co's *Directory of Hertfordshire* in the

The Fore Street, Hertford.

year of his death, 1832. The entry under *Hertford* states that this market town, 21 miles north of London, had the distinction of having sent two members to Parliament from the reign of Edward I, that the members are chosen by inhabitant householders and that the number of voters that year was about 650.

> The principle public buildings are the shire hall, situated in the Marketplace, comprising, in addition to the courts of law, a handsome assembly room. The town is lighted with gas. Letters from London arrive every night at half-past ten, and are despatched every morning at four.

Under the heading of "Nobility, Gentry and Clergy," there are 75 names, the fourth of which is:

> Barclay Captain, North Crescent[12]

A map in *The Victoria History of the County of Hertford* shows that North Crescent is a short section, comprised of 12 houses, of the road from Watton; the row of fine Georgian townhouses is still occupied, but it is not possible to determine which house once belonged to the Barkleys.

In 1823 the household was apparently thrown into consternation by the marriage of the oldest son, John Charles, to Mary Yarker. He married against the wishes of his parents and was "cut off" although they were later reconciled and John Charles became the executor of his mother's will. John Charles' first son, born in 1825, was given his grandmother's name: John *Trevor* Barkley. Another child, Edward, arrived in 1829.

Charles Barkley died in 1832 and was buried at Enfield, a town 12 miles south of Hertford, near London,

House in Hertford, possibly the Barkleys'.

Enfield Church.

where the entry in the church register notes that he was "formerly of this Parish." He was buried near his two sons, William Hippolyte Andrew (the boy who charmed the court in Cochin China) and the infant William. Walbran records a note from Frances' Diary: "On 16 May 1832, I lost my beloved husband, — in his 73rd year — worn out more by care and sorrow than by years, as he had been blessed with a very strong constitution."[13]

After Charles' death, Frances sold the tall house in Hertford and moved to Upper Clapton, a town near by. Family matters continued to concern her. Her son Charles Francis Barkley ran for Parliament, financed by his sister Jane Hornby Perkins, who sold a string of black pearls she had inherited from Ann Forbes, her godmother, to help pay her brother's campaign expenses. Charles wrote to Frances at Warwick Road, Upper Clapton, on January 7, 1835, to give a hastily scrawled account of the results:

All over

Barkley	Dundas	Lowther
920	1304	1501

Barkley and Dundas	900
Plumpers Dundas	101
Dundas & Lowther	<u>303</u>
	1304

Plumpers Lowther   1180
Won by the grossest bribery
400 deserters
will be a Petition
Expense not considerable
A very honorable contest for me
A piece of Plate is being subscribed for
£27 in the 1st room
Return certain if I ever stand again
Not in the least discouraged
Health improved I like to be beat in a good cause, it tells in the
  end
500 people literally have come to wish me good bye

Lowther does not show his nose.

C. F. B.[14]

In 1836, the year after the election excitement, and four years after
Charles' death, Frances began to write her *Reminiscences,* the fragmentary
and incomplete document published in this book. In 1841, at the age of 71,
she drafted a detailed will, naming as executors her oldest son, John Charles,
and her son-in-law Robert Grant Shaw, Martha's husband. Mary Jane Thurlow
(probably a servant, who had come to live with Frances) witnessed the document; George Husham Wynn, a neighbour and friend, added his signature.
In August of 1842, only a year after agreeing to execute her will, Robert
Shaw died. Chance has preserved a letter of sympathy from Frances' brother
Fred Trevor, demonstrating that her relationships with her half-brothers had
remained unbroken through the years:

> Exmouth, August 29, 1842
> My Dear Fanny,
> On my return last night from Otterton near Sidmouth
> which I served yesterday for the Archdeacon of Exeter, I found a
> letter from my brother John enclosing one from you detailing
> the melancholy account of poor Shaw's death, a terrible blow
> indeed for your daughter Patty. I sincerely condole with you
> both. I trust a kind Providence will afford you strength to bear
> so severe a calamity. I was in hopes that that dreadful pestilence
> had left us, & little thought that poor Shaw would fall a victim
> to it. My kindest love to both of you.
> For the last three years I have only been assisting my neigh-
> bours but have at length again accepted a care — the Sub-chap-
> laincy of the Church of St. Nicholas in Saltash near Plymouth
> wither I proceed tomorrow week.
> Pray remember me most kindly to poor Patty and her six
> children, more of whom I believe were born when I had last the
> pleasure of seeing her and believe me
> Your very affectionate brother
> Fred Trevor[15]

In September of that year Frances destroyed the sixth page of her will and substituted a new page appointing her grandson Edward Perkins as executor in place of Robert Shaw. It is worth enumerating the bequests of the will, in order to reveal the flourishing family who surrounded her in her last years, and to tell something of her prized possessions:

To her daughter Jane Hornby Perkins: a gold ring with Charles William Barkley's hair and 14 diamonds, a gold ring with Charles William Barkley's hair, and a black profile of Charles William Barkley.

To her second daughter Martha Shaw: a gold ring with sapphire, a gold brooch with sapphire, and drawings, paintings, miniatures.

To her second son Charles Francis Barkley: her small gold watch and chain, Charles Barkley's gold seal with his initials C. B., an antique watch, a gold seal with F. B., and a gold shirt pin with a pearl.

To granddaughter Frances Jane Perkins: a silver embossed teapot.

To granddaughter Amelia Sophia Perkins: A sable muff and boa.

To granddaughter Henrietta Perkins: a ruby hoop ring.

To Olivia Perkins: a gold locket.

To granddaughter Edith Perkins: £12 to purchase a watch.

To grandson Charles William Barkley: a large gold watch, also a heavy gold watch chain and gold seal with his grandfather's initials engraved.

To grandson and godson John Trevor Barkley: "his beloved grandfather's gold Chronometer or Time Piece … the said Chronometer to be kept by my said Executors until the said John Trevor Barkley shall have attained the age of twenty five years old when it is to be given to him with strict injunctions not to sell or otherwise dispose of it during his life time, it being my wish that the said Chronometer should be transmitted to his descendants or to some other branch of the family to be preserved as a memento of the estimation in which it was held by its late lamented owner during his long and perilous voyages whilst circumnavigating the Globe, it having been found to keep time under the influence of all climates. Also to the said John Trevor Barkley, a large gold seal with a white cornelian set therein with the arms of his family engraved thereon."

To grandson George Andrew Barkley: a profile of Uncle Andrew Barkley.

To grandson Edward Barkley: a red morocco pocket book.

To granddaughter Martha Barkley: £150 and a small gold locket with William Hippolyte Andrew's hair.

To granddaughter and goddaughter Frances Jane Barkley: £12 for a gold watch.

To grandson John Charles Barkley: Charles William Barkley's gold watch.

To granddaughter Emily Shaw: a silver embossed sugar basin.

To granddaughter Frances Martha Shaw: a gold chain or necklace with a gold locket with Charles William Barkley's hair and £12 for a watch.

To granddaughter Anna Shaw: £12 for a watch, and also a gold brooch with a Brighton pebble.

To granddaughter Clara Jane Shaw: a garnet hoop ring.

To granddaughter Annie Murray Barkley: a silver embossed cream ewer.

To Miss Mary Hunt "sister of John Hunt who died in the West Indies, Attorney at Law, and niece of Mrs. Prisilla Forbes": a miniature likeness of the lady. Also a legacy of thirty pound sterling.

To the daughters of her son John Charles: all trinkets not otherwise bequeathed, to be equally divided between them.

To son John Charles Barkley: all plate, China, ornaments, an eight-day clock, his father's antique ring, three likenesses in wood frames, also all household furniture and linens, all monies, debts and bonds.

In a codicil, Frances adds further bequests:

To Edward Perkins: £10 to purchase a ring.

To Mary Barkley, wife of John Charles Barkley: all wearing apparel, body linen and shawls.

To Jane Hornby Perkins: sundry pieces of old china as enumerated in the inventory.

To granddaughter Henrietta Perkins: a japanned card box and five boxes fitting in and counters.

To granddaughter Laura Shaw: "an ornamental cup and saucer now on the mantle shelf in the Drawing Room."

To Mary Jane Thurlow "now residing with me, a suit of clothes or the value of the same in money."[16]

With loving attention to each of her four children and 19 grandchildren, Frances allotted her possessions. Her precise instructions with regard to Charles' gold chronometer attempted to preserve the instrument and his memory for all time, but the present location of the chronometer is unknown.

Part of a letter survives, written in June or July of the next year, 1843, by widowed Martha Shaw upon settling at Cuckfield, Sussex. During the move much damage was done. Martha wrote to her mother, "I have resolved not to make myself unhappy about anything in this world except vital evils — otherwise to see so many breakages is very trying — imagine the beautiful old china vase, that very elegant one which was always under a glass case, broken. I have written to stop the old china coming and dread to see the next things unpacked."[17]

In September of that year Frances left Upper Clapton and went to live at Cuckfield with Martha, and two years later, in May of 1845, she died. She had asked in her will, "to be deposited in the Tomb with the remains of my late dear husband in Enfield Church yard, not to be interred with unnecessary pomp," and on May 30, her family carried out her order. It is probable that they all gathered for the funeral: Jane and Charles Perkins with their

Louise Barkley, a granddaughter of Frances.

five daughters, Frances Jane, Amelia Sophia, Henrietta, Olivia and Edith; John and Mary Barkley with John Trevor, Charles William, George Andrew, Edward and Frances Jane, as well as a Martha and a John Charles mentioned in Frances' will but not to be found on the family tree; the widow Martha Shaw with Emily, Frances Martha, Anna, Clara Jane and Laura; and Charles and Anne Barkley with ten-year-old Annie Murray Barkley, who was to be an only child because her father would die in that very year.

Today the roar of London is muted as one enters Enfield churchyard. Inside the ancient church, the secretary will open the vaults and produce the thick books recording burials. There may be found the brief entries which are the only proof that Frances and Charles and two of their sons (14-year-old William Hippolyte Andrew and the infant William) are buried in the churchyard, somewhere beneath the grass, in the shadow of old yew trees. No stone marks their graves.

The high adventures of the voyages are long past, their achievements forgotten. Yet the Barkleys are surely worthy of greater fame, for their adventures bring together all the different places and peoples of the world at a time when coasts were being charted, islands discovered and trade was opening up contact with new ideologies and cultures. Through Frances Barkley's eyes it is possible to catch a glimpse of the courageous mariners of the age of sail.

Enfield Church yard.

Her words draw a portrait of Charles, an honourable, warm and charming man with the intelligence and courage to rise to command, but she also wrote of the ruthless merchants and organization men whose only concern was their profits. Nothing further need be said about Frances herself, for her intrepid courage, her strength of character, intelligence and warmth are clearly revealed in the *Reminiscences,* even though she rarely speaks of herself. Above all, her words declare her devotion to her husband ... "I made up my mind to brave every danger rather than separate." At a time when Victorian society held a firm belief in female inferiority, her adventures were particularly remarkable. That her love was returned is clearly shown in Charles' letters to "Dearest Fanny." "Your kind and affectionate letters made me very happy on my arrival here," he wrote. "God for ever bless you, the best of women, and believe me, Your most Affectionate husband, Charles Barkley."[18]

One can imagine the *Imperial Eagle* lunging forward with the spray flying up, sparkling in the sun, the sails taut in the wind and the sea running. A thin line of jagged peaks lies along the horizon, a new land one day to be named Canada. The *Imperial Eagle* heels a little, the green sea curling white under her bows, and on her deck a woman stands braced against the joyous wind as she looks toward the distant coast, a woman with red-gold hair who deserves to be remembered.

Endnotes

Introduction

1. Cookson, R., in *How They Lived*, vol. 3, edited by Briggs, Asa. Oxford University Press, 1969, 51.
2. Boswell, J., *Life of Johnson*. 1791.
3. Berckman, E., *The Hidden Navy*. London, Hamish Hamilton, 1973, 7.
4. *Ibid.*, 18.
5. *Ibid.*, 34.

Chapter One: The Trevors and the Barkleys

1. Whereas the pound sterling was paramount throughout England, the Spanish silver dollar was the standard currency of trade. Calculating the equivalency between the two currencies is difficult due to market fluctuations: from 1619 to 1814, one pound roughly equalled four dollars.
2. British Columbia Archives, AA 30 B 242.
3. Parker, C., "Account of my Great Grandmother Miss Frances Trevor taken from her letters and her diary." Unpublished manuscript. 1913.
4. For this publication of Frances Barkley's *Reminiscences*, her spelling is unchanged, but punctuation has been added and the text broken into sentences and paragraphs. Spaces in text represent spaces in the manuscript.
5. Parker, *op.cit.*

6. An auction catalogue now in the British Museum records that on the 19th and 20th of March 1766 "the genuine house and furniture of John Trevor Esq." was sold at auction; there was enough furniture for a large house of "three reception rooms, four bedchambers, two attics, a kitchen and an office all in neat and good condition, the greatest part having been bought new within these nine months." In Trevor, H. E. "Doctor Trevor (A Phenomenon)," unpublished manuscript, 1913.

7. Paul, J. B., ed., *Scots Peerage*. Edinburgh, 1906. vol. III, 113-114.

8. *Ibid.*

9. Parker, *op. cit.*

10. Parker, *op. cit.*

11. East India Company (English). *Fort William-India House Correspondence*, vol. IV, 1764-1766, edited by C. S. Srinivasachari. Delhi, Civil Lines, 1962. Mar. 24, 1766, 412.

12. Ships' tonnage (capacity and size) was measured by the number of "tuns" of wine (each casked in two barrels of half a ton in weight) a ship could carry, each "tun" weighing about 2,240 pounds. A 400-ton ship could carry 400 tuns of wine, a fairly large vessel.

Chapter Two: The First Voyage: From Ostend to the Northwest Coast of North America

1. Smollett, T., *The Adventures of Roderick Random*. 1748, 204.

2. The Harmonicon which Frances remembered with delight proved to be so rare an instrument that no picture of it could be found. The name Harmonicon was first given to a series of musical glasses of graded size, the tones being produced by running wet fingers around the rims of the glasses. An early model of this instrument survives in the Horniman Museum in London, where there is also preserved the second version of the Musical Glasses, Benjamin Franklin's Armonica of 1737. Franklin heard a performance of the Musical Glasses and his quick mind produced the improved instrument, in which the glasses are nestled one inside the other on a spindle, so as to form a horizontal row; the spindle was then rotated by means of a treadle and the row of glasses turned in a shallow trough of water, so that the revolving rims were always wet and the player only touched them lightly to produce

the strange and unforgettable tones. Efforts to combine the Harmonicon with a keyboard produced an instrument with the glasses arranged in two rows and sounded by a series of levers, but no picture can be found of the German instrument of 1784, played for Frances Barkley in Brazil in 1787.

Chapter Three: The Northwest Coast of North America

1. Dixon, G., *A Voyage round the world, but more particularly to the northwest coast of America ... in the* King George *and* Queen Charlotte. London, Geo Goulding, 1789, 231-233.
2. Colnett, J., *A voyage to the South Atlantic and round Cape Horn into the Pacific Ocean.* Amsterdam, N. Israel, 1968.
3. The British Columbia Archives has also preserved a clipping in the John T. Walbran file entitled "Scrapbook of Miscellaneous cuttings 1909-1912" in which Walbran wrote: "It was Capt. Barkley's voyage and the claim he acquired to land at Nootka by bargain with the Indians, which was the foundation of the British claim to this part of the world, although later Capt. Meares came to occupy a more conspicuous position in the controversy." Walbran may have found this information in Frances Barkley's Diary, and it is possible that it was this item which caused her son to forward Captain Barkley's Journal to the Earl of Aberdeen at the time of the Oregon Boundary Dispute.
4. Meares, J., *Voyages made in the years 1788 and 1789 from China to the North-west Coast of America.* London, Logographic Press, 1790, 171.
5. Walbran, J. T., *British Columbia Coast Names.* Vancouver, J.J. Douglas, 1971, 274.
6. Cook, J. and King. J., *A Voyage to the Pacific Ocean.* London, G. Nicol and T. Cadell, 1784. vol. II, 263.
7. Meares, *op. cit.*

Chapter Four: China

1. Barbeau, M., *Pathfinders in the North Pacific.* Toronto, Ryerson Press, 1958.
2. Barabash-Nikijorov, I. I., *The Sea Otter.* London, Oldbourne Press, 1962.

3. Meares, J., *Voyages made in the years 1788 and 1789 ...* 171, 241.

4. Cook, J. and King, J. *A Voyage to the Pacific Ocean.*

5. Ginseng is a plant whose roots (two to three inches long) are used, mainly by the Chinese, as a stimulant and tonic and to lengthen their lives. A most fastidious plant, the ginseng grows in shady places, requires virgin soil and grows slowly, although it may live to be from 30 to 60 years old. Many roots have a peculiar resemblance to the human form and these are carried by the Chinese as charms. Most ginseng comes from Korea and Manchuria but it is also found in America. As 400,000,000 Chinese all to some extent use ginseng, it is an important import.

6. Dixon, G., *A Voyage round the world*, 289.

7. Meares, *op. cit.*, 27.

Chapter Five: Mauritius and the End of the First Voyage

1. The value of the Barkley sale is given in Spanish dollars, invoiced at around five shillings per dollar.

2. Walbran, J. T., *British Columbia Coast Names*, 34.

3. Parker, C., "Account of my Great Grandmother Miss Frances Trevor taken from her letters and her diary." Unpublished manuscript. 1913.

4. Quoted in Toussaint, A., *Port Louis a tropical city.* W. E. F. Ward, translator, London, Allen & Unwin, 1973, 5.

5. Prosser, I. E., Letter to Constance Parker, March 17, 1934. British Columbia Archives. Cecil Denne lived in Vancouver, and probably read the Diary when it was still at Westholme on Vancouver Island.

6. Walbran, J. T., "The Cruise of the *Imperial Eagle*." *Victoria Colonist*, March 3, 1901, 27.

7. Haswell, R., *Voyages of the* Columbia *to the Northwest Coast 1787-1790 and 1790-1793*, edited by Frederic W. Howay. Massachusetts Historical Society, 1941.

8. Dixon, G., *Remarks on the Voyages of John Meares, Esq.* London, 1790, 8.

9. *Ibid.*, 7.

10. *Ibid.*, 31.

11. *Ibid.*, 12.

12. *Ibid.*, 33.

13. *Ibid.*, 34.

14. Howay, F. W., *The Dixon-Meares Controversy*. Toronto, Ryerson, 1929, 22.
15. Meares, *Voyages made in the years 1788 and 1789 ...* 151.
16. *Ibid.*, 155.
17. *Ibid.*, 169.
18. *Ibid.*, 171.
19. Dixon, *op. cit.*, 36.
20. Parker, *op. cit.*

Chapter Six: India: The Second Voyage Begins

1. Parker, C., "Account of my Great Grandmother Miss Frances Trevor taken from her letters and her diary." Unpublished manuscript. 1913. Constance Parker undoubtedly intended to write Cape of Good Hope, not Cape Horn, in the sentence which tells of the birth of the second child, Martha.
2. Fort William-India House Correspondence, April 27, 1792.
3. Boobies: any of several gannets (genus Sala) of the tropical seas, resembling the common gannet but smaller.
4. A lead weight on the end of a marked line was used for measuring the depth of water. A seaman whirled the lead and dropped it into the sea ahead of the ship, then pulled it in and whirled it again for another cast. The depth was read from markers attached to the line, and the seaman must recognize by feel a piece of calico, a bit of leather with a hole in it, etc. It was exhausting work, and the leadsman would be soaking wet from spray, and from hauling in the dripping line, and sometimes he would be so chilled that his numb fingers would drop the line, as happened aboard the *Princess Frederica* on this occasion.
5. Parker, *op. cit.* Mrs. Forbes was not Captain Barkley's aunt Ann Barkley. The Mr. Forbes the Barkleys visited in Calcutta was James Forbes, Charles Barkley's first cousin. James was the son of Ann Barkley, sister of Charles' father. James Forbes subsequently left a portion of his fortune to Charles and his children.
6. Quoted in Moorhouse, G., *Calcutta*. London, Weidenfeld & Nicolson, 1971, 17.
7. *Ibid.*, 36.
8. *Ibid.*, 51.

9. The two dates are written in a paler ink, obviously filled in at a later date.
10. Sillabub: a dish made of milk or cream mixed with wine, cider or the like, often sweetened and flavoured.
11. Sauer, M., *An account of a geographical & astronomical expedition to the northern parts of Russia … in the years 1785-1794*. London, T. Cadell, 1802, 277. William Barkley was four years old at this time, not seven.

Chapter Seven: Alaska, Hawaii and Cochin China

1. Holmberg, H.I., quoted in Krause, A., *The Tlingit Indians*. Seattle, University of Washington Press, 1956, 98.
2. Menzies' *Journal* gives a list of vessels on the northwest coast of America in the year 1792. Although no Captain Hancock is mentioned, there is a brig *Hancock*, an American ship from China whose captain was named Crowell. Recorded by Howay is the further information that Crowell and Creighton's brigantine *Hancock* sailed from Boston in November 1790, and arrived on the coast in July 1791, after an eventful passage via Cape Horn and the Hawaiian Islands. She sailed to China in the autumn of 1791 and returned to the coast in 1792 and 1793. No mention is made of the abandonment of four men on the Alaskan coast.
3. According to Walbran, Frances Barkley's Diary ended at this word.
4. Cook, J. and King, J. *A Voyage to the Pacific Ocean*. London, G. Nicol and T. Cadell, 1784. II.
5. Vancouver, G., *A Voyage of Discovery to the North Pacific Ocean*. London, G. G. and J. Robinson, 1798.
6. Barrow, J., *A Voyage to Cochinchina*. Oxford University Press, 1975. Originally published 1806, 246.
7. Walbran, J.T., "The Cruise of the *Imperial Eagle*." *Victoria Colonist*, March 3, 1901, 27.

Chapter Eight: The Barkleys in England

1. Barkley, Frances Jane., Letter to Constance Parker from Hethersett, September 4, 1913.
2. Barkley-Denne, Alured., Errata in Barkley tree sent to City of Vancouver

Archives, Vancouver, B.C.

3. Barkley, Charles William., Letter to Frances Barkley from Dublin. May 23, 1808.

4. Barkley, C. W., Letter to John Barkley from Buenos Aires. Undated.

5. Barkley, C. W., Letter to Frances Barkley from Bridlington, August 17, 1810.

6. *Ibid.*

7. Barkley, C. W., Letter to Frances Barkley from Cromarty, August 23, 1810.

8. Barkley, C. W., Letter to Frances Barkley from Cromarty, August 24, 1810.

9. Barkley, C. W., Letter to Frances Barkley from Cromarty, August 27, 1810.

10. Barkley, C. W., Letter to Frances Barkley from Cromarty, August 29, 1810.

11. Barkley, C. W., Letter to John Barkley from Buenos Aires. Undated.

12. Pigot & Co's *Directory*. Hertfordshire, 1832.

13. Walbran, J. T., *British Columbia Coast Names*, 35.

14. Barkley, Charles Francis., Letter to Frances Barkley. January 7, 1835.

15. Trevor, Frederic, Letter to Frances Barkley from Exmouth. August 29, 1842.

16. Barkley, Frances Hornby Trevor, Will. Public Record Office, Chancery Lane, London. 1841.

17. Shaw, Martha, Letter to Frances Barkley from Cuckfield. Browsholme Hall, Lancashire. 1843.

18. Barkley, C. W., Letter to Frances Barkley from Cromarty. August 23, 1810.

Sources

Unpublished

Aberdeen, Earl of. January 1846. Letter to John Charles Barkley. Copy, British Columbia Archives. M B 242.

Barkley, Charles Francis. January 7, 1835. Letter to Frances Barkley. Frederica Barkley.

Barkley, Charles William. 1786-1793. A Journal of the proceedings on board the *Loudoun*. British Columbia Archives. AA 20.5 L 92.

_____. 1787–1792. Logbook, no title. Includes journal of proceedings on board the brig *Halcyon*, and log of the ship *Princess Frederica*, May 8, 1791–August 25, 1791. British Columbia Archives. AA 20.5 H 12 B.

_____. May 23, 1808. Letter to Frances Barkley from Dublin. Copy, Frederica Barkley.

_____. August 17, 1810. Letter to Frances Barkley from Bridlington. Copy, Robert J. Barkley.

_____. August 23, 1810. Letter to Frances Barkley from Cromarty. Copy, Robert J. Barkley.

_____. August 24, 1810. Letter to Frances Barkley from Cromarty. Frederica Barkley.

_____. August 27, 1810. Letter to Frances Barkley from Cromarty. Copy, Robert J. Barkley.

_____. August 29, 1810. Letter to Frances Barkley from Cromarty. Copy, Robert J. Barkley.

_____. September 5, 1810. Letter to Frances Barkley from Edinburgh. Copy, Robert J. Barkley.

_____. Undated. Letter to John Barkley from Buenos Aires. British Columbia Archives. A A 30 B 242.

_____ and Frances Trevor. Marriage certificate. 1786. Copy, Guildhall Library, London.

Barkley, Edith Perkins. August 10, 1911. Letter to A. S. Scholefield. British Columbia Archives. MB 242.

Barkley, Edward (?). Undated note summarizing Charles William Barkley's early voyages. British Columbia Archives. M B 242.

Barkley, Frances Hornby Trevor. April 6, 1769. Baptismal record, photographed in St. Mary's Church, Bridgwater, Somerset.

_____. 1791. Two sheets from a journal: a. A clothes list for the voyage of the *Halcyon*, and b. Journal page which corresponds approximately with p. 27 of the transcript of the *Reminiscences*. British Columbia Archives. A A 20 B 24.1.

_____. 1793. Twelve journal pages describing visit in Cochinchina. British Columbia Archives. A A 20 B 24.

_____. 1836. Reminiscences. G. B. Barnes, on loan to the British Columbia Archives. A A 30 B 24.

_____. 1841. Will. Public Record Office, Chancery Lane, London.

Barkley, Frances Jane. September 4, 1913. Letter to Constance Parker from Hethersett, Norwich. Browsholme Hall, Lancashire.

Barkley, John Charles. August 29, 1833. Letter to Frances Barkley. Frederica Barkley.

_____. January 1846. Letter to the Earl of Aberdeen. Copy in British Columbia Archives. MB 242.

Barkley, Robert Edward. February 28, 1934. Letter to Constance Parker. British Columbia Archives. MB 242.

_____. 1914. Letter. British Columbia Archives. MB 242.

Barkley-Denne, Alured. Errata in Barkley family tree sent to City of Vancouver Archives, Vancouver. Major V. A. H. Denne.

Genealogical Table of the Ancient Family of Hampden. Whitminster House, Gloucestershire.

Howay, Frederic William. An Outline Sketch of the Maritime Fur Trade. Presidential address presented at the annual Canadian Historical

Association. 1932.

Otterhampton Church, List of Rectors. Otterhampton, Somerset.

Parker, Constance. 1913. Account of my Great Grandmother Miss Frances Trevor taken from her letters and her diary. Browsholme Hall, Lancashire.

_____. 1928. Letter to Florence Teesdale, Gloucester. Copy, British Columbia Archives. MB 242.

_____. March 21, 1934. Letter to Robert E. Barkley, of Westholme, British Columbia Archives. MB 242.

_____. July 18, 1934. Letter to Robert E. Barkley. British Columbia Archives. MB 242.

_____. July 21, 1934. Letter to Robert E. Barkley. British Columbia Archives. MB 242.

Prosser, Ida E. March 17, 1934. Letter to Constance Parker. British Columbia Archives. MB 242.

Shaw, Martha. 1843. Letter to Frances Barkley from Cuckfield. Browsholme Hall, Lancashire.

Trevor, Frederic. August 29, 1842. Letter to Frances Barkley from Exmouth. Frederica Barkley.

Trevor, Henry Edward. April 1913. "Doctor Trevor (A Phenomenon)." Incomplete document. Frederica Barkley.

Tyler, Ada Perkins. October 17 (year unknown). Letter to Constance Parker. Browsholme Hall, Lancashire.

_____. 1913. Letter to Constance Parker. British Columbia Archives. MB 242.

Vyvyan, Frances Claire Perkins. No date. Letter to Constance Parker. Browsholme Hall, Lancashire.

Walbran, John T. November 22, 1909. Note taken from Mrs. Barkley's Journal. British Columbia Archives. M B 242.

Published

Allom, Thomas and G.H. Wright. *China, in a series of views*. London, Fisher, Son & Co., 1843.

Barabash-Nikiforov, I. I. *The Sea Otter*. London, Oldbourne Press, 1962.

Barbeau, Marius. *Pathfinders in the North Pacific*. Toronto, Ryerson Press. 1958.

Barrow, John. *A Voyage to Cochinchina.* Oxford University Press reprint. 1975.

Beaglehole, J. C. *The Voyage of the* Resolution *and* Discovery *1776-1780.* Cambridge University Press.

Berckman, Evelyn. *The Hidden Navy.* London, Hamish Hamilton. 1973.

Boswell, James. *Life of Johnson.* 1791.

Briggs, Asa, ed. *How They Lived.* vol. 3 (1700-1815). Oxford University Press. 1969.

Busteed, H. E. *Echoes from old Calcutta.* London, W. Thacker & Co. 1908.

City of Vancouver Archives. *The Founders of Vancouver.* Pamphlet in commemoration of the seventieth anniversary of the incorporation of Vancouver as a city, May 1956.

Colnett, James. *A voyage to the South Atlantic and round Cape Horn into the Pacific Ocean.* London, A. Arrowsmith *et al.* Reprinted by N. Israel, Amsterdam. 1968.

Cook, James and James King. *A Voyage to the Pacific Ocean.* 3 vols. London, G. Nicol and T. Cadell. 1784.

Director General Canadian Hydrographic Service. *Sailing Directions British Columbia Coast South Portion.* Ottawa, Department of Fisheries and Oceans. 1999.

Dixon, George. A. *A Voyage Round the World ... performed in 1785, 1786, 1787 and 1788.* London, Geo. Goulding. Reprinted by N. Israel, Amsterdam and Da Capo Press, New York. 1968.

———. *Remarks on the Voyages of John Meares Esq. in a letter to that gentleman.* London. 1790.

Durett, Joan. *Hen Frigates.* New York, Touchstone. 1998.

East India Company (English). *Fort William–India House Correspondence,* vol. IV, 1764-1766. C. S. Srinivasachari, ed. Delhi, Civil Lines. 1962.

———. *Fort William- India House Correspondence.* vol. XVII, 1792. C. S. Srinivasachari, ed. Delhi, Civil Lines. 1962.

Elliott, G. R. *Empire and Enterprise in the North Pacific, 1785-1825.* University of Toronto thesis. 1957.

Forrest, Thomas. *A Voyage to New Guinea and the Moluccas 1774-1776.* Oxford University Press reprint. 1969.

Gough, Barry. *The Northwest Coast: British Navigation Trade and Discoveries to 1812.* Vancouver, University of British Columbia Press. 1992.

Haswell, Robert. *Voyages of the* Columbia *to the Northwest Coast, 1787-1790 and 1790-1793.* Frederic W. Howay, ed. Massachusetts Historical Society. 1941.

Howay, Frederic William. *The Dixon-Meares Controversy.* Toronto, Ryerson Press. 1929.

_____. *List of trading vessels in Maritime fur trade, 1785-1825.* Ottawa, Royal Society of Canada. 1930.

Krause, Aurel. *The Tlingit Indians.* Seattle, University of Washington Press. 1956.

Lamb, W. Kaye. "The Mystery of Mrs. Barkley's Diary." *British Columbia Historical Journal,* vol. V1, no. 1, January. 1942.

Meares, John. *Voyages made in the years 1788 and 1789, from China to the North west coast of America, ...* London, Logographic Press. 1790.

Menzies, Archibald. *Menzies' Journal of Vancouver's Voyage, April to October 1792.* C. F. Newcombe, ed. (British Columbia Archives, Memoir no. V). Victoria, W. H. Cullin. 1923.

Miller, Russell. *The East Indiamen.* Virginia, Time-Life Books. 1980.

Moorhouse, Geoffrey. *Calcutta.* London, Weidenfeld & Nicolson. 1971.

Paul, J. Balfour, ed. *Scots Peerage.* v. 111. Edinburgh. 1906.

Sauer, Martin. *An account of a geographical & astronomical expedition to the northern parts of Russia ... in the years 1785-1794.* London, printed by A. Straban for T. Cadell Jnr. & W. Davies, in the Strand. 1802.

Smollett, Tobias. *The Adventures of Roderick Random.* London, reprinted by Oxford University Press. 1930.

Staunton, George. *Authentic account of an embassy from the King of Great Britain to the Emperor of China.* London, G. Nicol. 1798.

Sutton, Jean. *Lords of the East: The East India Company and its Ships (1600-1874).* 2nd ed. London, Conway Maritime Press. 2000.

Todd, J. and W.B. Whall. *Practical Seamanship for Use in the Merchant Service.* London, George Philip & Son. 1980.

Toussaint, A.. *Port Louis.* London, George Allen & Unwin Ltd. 1973.

Vancouver, George. *A Voyage of Discovery to the North Pacific Ocean.* London, G. G. & J. Robinson. 1798.

Walbran, John T. "The Cruise of the *Imperial Eagle.*" In the *Victoria Colonist,* March 3, 1901.

_____ *British Columbia Coast Names 1592-1906.* Vancouver, J.J. Douglas. 1971.

Notes on the Sources

When Frances died in 1845, the Diary, the *Reminiscences,* Charles Barkley's Journal and the logbooks were left to her oldest son, John Charles Barkley. The following year he offered "the logbook and journal in Capt. Barkley's handwriting"[1] to the Earl of Aberdeen, as evidence of British rights on the northwest coast of North America in the Oregon Boundary Dispute: "My mother, who was the companion of my father in that voyage, only died this last summer and the above papers, which since my Father's decease had never been out of her hands, then came into my possession,"[2] he wrote to the earl. The offer was accepted, and it is possible that Charles Barkley's Journal and the missing sections of the logbooks disappeared at that time.

The Diary next passed to Frances' granddaughter, Frances Jane Barkley. In about 1900 she loaned it to her brother, Captain Edward Barkley, who had settled at Westholme on Vancouver Island. Edward Barkley showed it to Captain John T. Walbran who then used it for his 1909 publication *British Columbia Coast Names.*[3] Walbran also published an account of the Barkley voyage in the *Victoria Colonist* in 1901, entitled "The Cruise of the *Imperial Eagle,*"[4] which is reprinted in Chapter Three of this book. Not long after Walbran had returned the precious document to Westholme, in November of 1909, Captain Edward Barkley's house burned to the ground. A Victoria newspaper reported:

> The fire broke out in the early morning when Capt. Barkley and a Chinese were alone in the building, and both escaped. Capt. Barkley then remembered something he wanted to save and went back. He made one trip in safety then returned again but this time did not emerge and his charred body was found in the ruins of the house.[5]

On his first return to the burning house, Captain Barkley brought out a leather case containing papers and placed this on the porch. When it was found by neighbours, the leather box was partially destroyed and the papers in it had been reduced to ashes. The newspapers of the day, and historians at a later date, concluded that Frances Barkley's Diary had been destroyed.

There is, however, some evidence that the Diary was not burned. The coincidental appearance of Miss Barlow at Whitminster House and her evidence has already been described. A letter from Robert Edward Barkley (son of the old gentleman who died in the burning house) to Constance Parker (a great-granddaughter of Frances Barkley) states:

> this Diary, which the Great Grandmother wrote some years after her visit to B.C., in fact she must have been quite old. Years ago when my Father (Capt. Edward Barkley) was alive, Aunt Fan sent either this Diary or another out here to him and he lent it to a Capt. Waldroon — *That Diary was sent back to Aunt Fan* [italics added] — after Aunt Fan's death Uncle Bob's wife Aunt Katie, sent me the one I have. I have put it in the Archives on loan — for safe keeping.[6]

Captain Edward Barkley, who died in the fire at Westholme, Vancouver Island.

The document Robert E. Barkley placed in the Archives was the original of the *Reminiscences,* published for the first time in this book. It would appear from his letter that the Diary of 1786-1792 had been sent back to England. Among the Barkley letters in the British Columbia Archives is one from Edith Barkley (sister-in-law of Edward who died in the fire) to A. S. Scholefield, provincial librarian of British Columbia, stating, "I will have the diary copied and will send you the copy shortly. The original diary is very much mixed up with family matters and I will go through it and have the portions copied which deal with our Grandfather and Grandmother's voyages .... The Diary belongs to me personally."[7] Edith Perkins Barkley died in 1919. It is not known whether she had the copy made, but no such document has been found.

The archives also preserves some letters from Constance Parker (1857-1937),[8] who in 1934 needed the Diary of 1786 for genealogical evidence and

Constance Parker.

was bitterly disappointed when the British Columbia Archives held only the *Reminiscences*. Research at Browsholme Hall, Lancashire, Constance Parker's home, uncovered "An account of my Great Grandmother Miss Frances Trevor, taken from her letters and her Diary ... copied by me, 1913, Constance Parker of Waddington." This document of 1913 must have been based on the *Reminiscences,* since Constance Parker was avidly seeking the Diary in 1934. The iron box of family papers at Browsholme also contained an undated letter from Lady Frances Vyvyan which included this sentence:

> I have also in my possession the Diary of Frances Barkley in which she mentions her daughter Jane, — so that may reveal something when I look it up. I expect you have seen that diary at some date, but if not I could lend it to you later on to look at.[9]

As the *Reminiscences* do not refer to daughter Jane, it is possible that the Diary of 1786 had descended through another family line to Lady Frances Vyvyan who died in 1952. To date it has not been found among the papers of her heirs, as far as it has been possible to trace them, and it may have been casually loaned by Lady Vyvyan to some friend and so lost.

As for the logs of the voyages, a few fragments are preserved in two bound volumes in the British Columbia Archives.[10] These books, purchased by Judge Howay in London and subsequently acquired by the archives, contain the following sections:

Volume 1: 1. Ship *Loudoun* from Ostend toward Brazil, Nov. 24, 1786-June 11, 1787

2. Brig *Halcyon* from St. Peter & St. Paul towards Behrings Straits, July 20, 1792-December 24, 1792

3. Brig *Halcyon* from China to Cochin China, Feb. 25, 1793-March 6, 1793

4. Brig *Halcyon* from Cochin China towards Mauritius, March 24-June 6, 1793

Volume 2: 1. Brig *Halcyon* from Bengal to the Coast of Northwest America, January 7-July 19, 1792

Browsholme Hall, Lancashire, home of Constance Parker.

2. Ship *Diana*, November 10, 1787-February 12, 1788
3. Ship *Warren Hastings* November 26, 1787-January 13, 1788
4. Ship *Princess Frederica,* Copenhagen to Bombay, May 8, 1791-August 25, 1791

It will be observed that the books consist of a number of sections bound together, for the dates are out of order and in the second volume, the middle two sections are parts of the logs of ships under the command of Charles Barkley's older brother, John. It has not been possible to discover at what date or by whose hand these volumes were compiled. The existing sections of log record facts concerning the weather, the route and the condition of the vessels but they tell almost nothing of events aboard ship. However, they have proved useful to connect some events recorded in the *Reminiscences* and other documents, and are extensively quoted in the present account.

From all these sources, and from general information and references to the Barkleys in the writings of their contemporaries, a fairly complete account has been pieced together.

Endnotes to Notes on the Sources

1. Barkley, J. C., Letter to the Earl of Aberdeen, 1846. British Columbia Archives.
2. *Ibid.*
3. Walbran, J. T., *British Columbia Coast Names, 1592-1906.* Vancouver, J.J. Douglas, 1971.
4. Walbran, J. T., "The Cruise of the *Imperial Eagle.*" *Victoria Colonist,* March 3, 1901.
5. *Victoria Colonist,* November 23, 1909.
6. Barkley, R. E., Letter to Constance Parker, February 28, 1934. British Columbia Archives.
7. Barkley, E., Letter to A. S. Scholefeld, August 10, 1911. British Columbia Archives.
8. Parker, C., "Account of my Great Grandmother Miss Frances Trevor taken from her letters and her diary." Unpublished manuscript. 1913.
9. Vyvyan, F., Letter to Constance Parker. Undated. Browsholme Hall, Lancashire.
10. Barkley, C. W., A Journal of the Proceedings on board the *Loudoun.* British Columbia Archives. AA 20.5 L 92. Barkley, C. W. Untitled. Including Journal of proceedings on board the brig *Halcyon.* British Columbia Archives. AA 20.5 H 12 B.

Credits

The original maps were drawn by T. T. Jarvie, Victoria, BC, and have been adapted by Katherine Hale.

Every effort has been made to contact the owners of copyrighted images. These illustrations appear by the courtesy of the following individuals, companies and institutions:

Frontispiece, ii: detail from the original cover painting by Harry Heine;
Constance, Lady Parker (portrait), 15: E.C. Parker;
Bridgwater, 17: Admiral Blake Museum, Bridgwater;
John Trevor, 20, Charles William Barkley, 25, Andrew Barkley, 163, John
    Charles Barkley, 173, Louise Barkley, 181 and Constance, Lady Parker
    (standing), 198: Roger Parker;
Indiaman, 28: Science Museum, London;
Winee, 40: N. Israel;
the *Imperial Eagle*, 44, painting by Steve Mayo: Steve Mayo;
drawings by John Webber, 46, 52, clothing list for the *Halcyon*, 96, page
    of logbook, 105, page of Diary, 114, Port Mulgrave chief, 130, Port
    Mulgrave man, 133 and page of *Reminiscences*, 149: BC Archives;
pictures of Macao, 64, 65, Whampoa, 66 and Canton, 67-69: Miles
    Acheson;
the Barkley chair, 70: Centennial Museum, Vancouver, BC;

Avacha Bay, 111, 119: Oregon Historical Society, Portland, OR;
Tlingit basket, 135 and James Forbes, 169: Frederica and Hermione
    Barkley;
Cochin Chinese shipping, 151: Oxford University Press;
Fore Street, 174: Hertford Museum;
Captain Edward Barkley, 197: Commander G.B. Barnes.

Index